HAPPY DAYS

A Pictorial History of
Toddington Schools
with Informative Text and Anecdotes

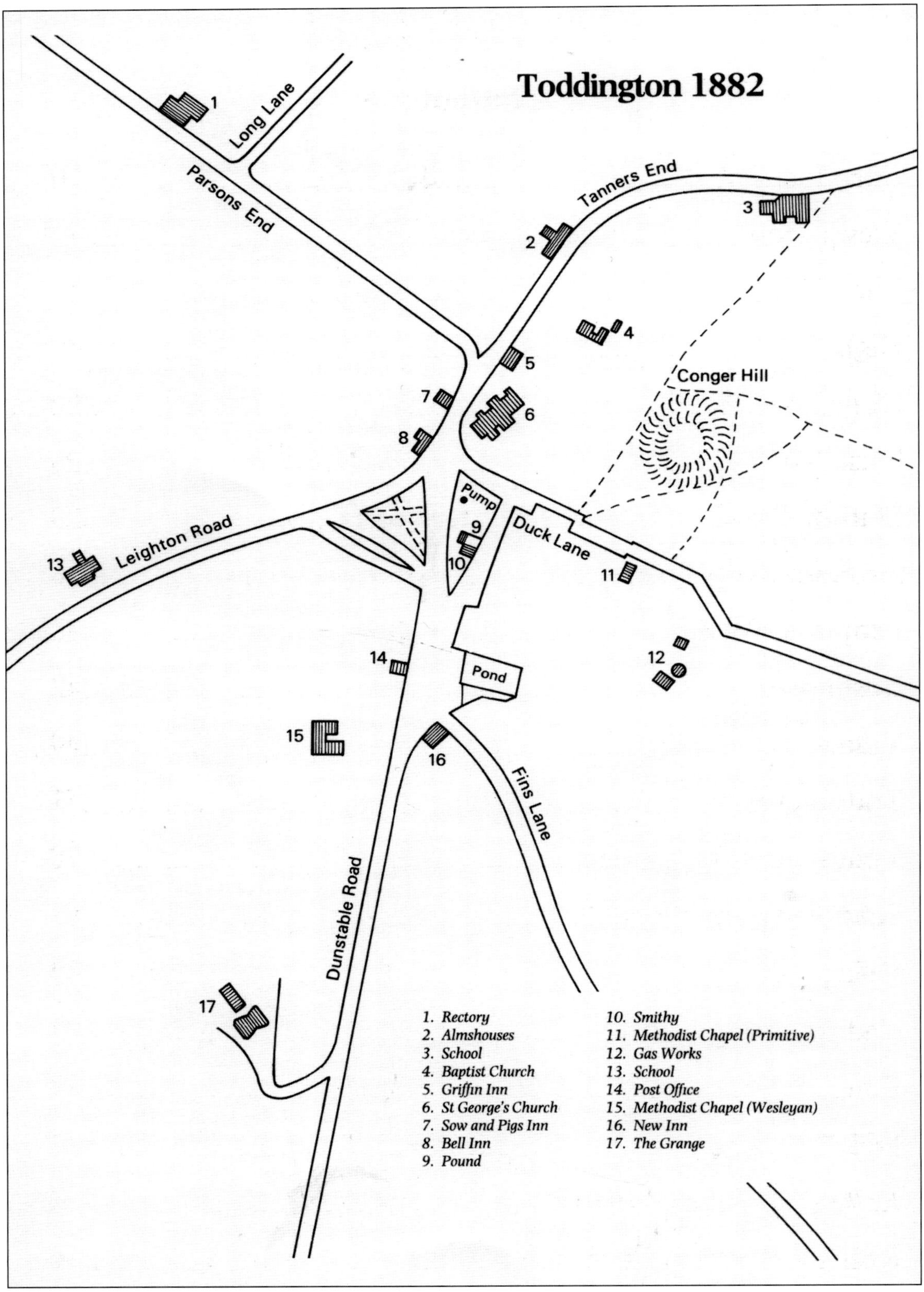
Toddington 1882
Long Lane
Parsons End
Tanners End
Conger Hill
Pump
Duck Lane
Leighton Road
Pond
Fins Lane
Dunstable Road
1
2
3
4
5
6
7
8
9
10
11
12
13
14
15
16
17
1. Rectory
2. Almshouses
3. School
4. Baptist Church
5. Griffin Inn
6. St George's Church
7. Sow and Pigs Inn
8. Bell Inn
9. Pound
10. Smithy
11. Methodist Chapel (Primitive)
12. Gas Works
13. School
14. Post Office
15. Methodist Chapel (Wesleyan)
16. New Inn
17. The Grange

HAPPY DAYS

A Pictorial History of Toddington Schools with Informative Text and Anecdotes

Compiled by
Richard Hart

Limited Edition

F B
Farnon Books

List of Illustrations

All the pictures have been supplied by the Toddington Old Boys Association apart from those listed below:

Bedfordshire & Luton Archives Service: 48, 53, 116b, 117, 119
Beds Magazine: 14
Bedfordshire Times: 60ab, 62b
Beryl Hyde Collection: 25ab, 26ab, 29a, 51ab, 54a, 55ab, 64a, 66b, 75b, 115b
John Bryant: 69
David Calcott: 131a, 157ab, 158ab, 159a
Wendy Chapman: 87
Jo Cross: 156b
Dunstable Gazette: 52a
Carol Gibbs: 81a
Home Counties Newspapers Ltd: 13b, 19, 34a, 44a, 49ab, 70, 79ab, 81b
Harold Keech: 106ab
Edna Kent: 29b
Kestral Studios: 155ab
Luton Herald: 104a
Luton News: 159b
Tom Shepherd: 36b, 39b, 46, 47, 52b, 103ab
Pat Smith: 80a
Post and Echo: 130b
Margaret Uff: 44b
John Wren: 28a

(a:above; b:below)

Published by
Farnon Books
Leighton Buzzard

Typeset by
GCS, Leighton Buzzard

Printed by
Berforts Information Press Ltd
Stevenage

ISBN: 978-0-9511698-6-5

Contents

Preface

The aim of this book has been to capture the atmosphere of the times by using pictures with informative text. There is a wealth of detail and a fund of anecdotes to make mellow a rainy day. Every picture has a caption, plus an index of National and Primary School pupils from 1917 to 1961 together with a list of teachers and headteachers. The photographs which have been selected should bring back happy memories and a smile. I hope you enjoy them, too.

All reasonable efforts have been made to find copyright holders for any illustrations used. In addition every effort has been made to accurately transcribe hand-written names and to correctly identify the individuals in the photographs. To a large extent the memory of others has been relied upon to identify individuals in the pictures. Where errors have been made they will be corrected by way of an erratum.

Acknowledgements

I am particularly indebted to so many former pupils and teachers. It is impossible for me to include the names of all the people who have provided facts and details but I would like to thank the following:

Beds and Luton Archives and Records Service, Linda Boylen, John Bryant, David Buckingham, David Calcott, Lesley Clements, Hedley and Joanna Denmark, Harold Fletcher, Debbie Gibbons, Jackie Harper, Beryl Hyde, Len Hull, Luton News, Isabel McLellan, David Morgan, Susan Riley, Aubrey Russell , June Smith, Rita Stares, Tom Shepherd, Lesly Squires, Margaret Uff, Jill Ward, Sally Ward and Jill Whitfield.

I would also like to thank several people who have been especially helpful in reading though the text and offering observations on it, in particular Christine and Roy Baker, Maureen and Paul Brown, David Calcott, Dee Curtis, Priscilla Hart and Tom Shepherd.

Richard Hart

Toddington Schools

The first recorded school in Toddington was in 1652 which was held in the Church House known today as the former Town Hall. References have been found to two headteachers in the 18th century and to a William Horley, described as 'headmaster' in 1851.

In 1818 a House of Commons Select Committee sent a circular letter to every parish enquiring about the educational provision for the poor. Edward Lewis, Toddington rector, completed the return and stated the population was 1,182 and that the poor 'are desirous of the means of education'. The return stated 'A Sunday School, open to all the parish, supported by voluntary subscription, established in 1815, in which 99 boys and 93 girls are instructed; there are three masters , one at 10s a month, the other two at 8s; a day school, containing 38 boys and 10 girls; and one belonging to the Baptists consisting of 38 children.'

By 1833 the population had increased to 1,926. Surprisingly 'five Daily Schools now existed, two containing 20 males and 15 females (of the Established Church); one containing 24 females; another, 30 males and 5 females (Baptist Dissenters); and the last contains six males and 25 females (Wesleyan Methodists). All these schools were supported by payments from parents. The rector allowed £6 10s for teaching several poor boys to write; 40 of the above scholars also attended the Sunday Schools of which there were four; one of the Established Church, in which 54 males and 86 females, conducted by two teachers who respectively receive £6 10s and £5 4s yearly, arising from subscription; one, supported by Baptist Dissenters, contains 20 males and 31 females; and the other two schools (Wesleyan Methodists) contain 128 males and 136 females; the three last mentioned schools were supported by subscription.' The Wesleyans seemed to be winning the competition for the best school.

The Church of England (Established Church), Baptist Dissenters and Wesleyan Methodists were all competing for pupils. At this time providing education for children was a way of recruiting their parents into the church. Parents also attended at evenings and weekends to learn to read and write themselves. Learning to read and write was a way to a better life. In 1864 the rector of Toddington highlighted the problems faced by the adults. He wrote: 'Hardly one young man or woman can write even their own name; the marriage registers can prove this. Very few can read, judging by the congregation at church, very few of whom use a prayer book. Vast numbers of young men and women are to be seen and heard loitering about the lanes at night and especially on Sundays. Their morals are at a very low ebb. A large average of the women have illegitimate children, and some at such an early age as quite to startle even those who are at home in criminal statistics.'

Education varied enormously. For example Dame Schools were small private schools that provided an education for working class children before they were old enough to work. Fees were about 3d per week and the quality of education varied enormously. Some provided a good education but many were run by one ill trained woman in a room in her house. She was generally poor herself and not really a trained teacher. Here the children didn't learn much more than the alphabet and how to sew.

Plaiting schools were set up around 1800 in the South Midlands area to help meet the growing demand for plait. Around Toddington straw of a suitable quality was grown and farmers were anxious to supply it in a condition ready to plait as an additional source of income. Children were sent to Plait Schools, where for the payment of 2d a week, boys and girls did straw plait and received an 'education'. Their mothers taught them to plait before they went to school and the women who kept the school mostly supervised the work and there was little education. What education there was varied enormously. Some 'teachers' were good but others were illiterate. Children were meant to receive a basic education as well as produce a given amount of plait daily in order that their mothers could continue to sew hats at home. All this added to the much needed family income. The children would be expected to earn nine pence a week aged eight and as much as three shillings a week by the age of fourteen. The Overseers of the Poor encouraged these activities, so that the Poor Rate might be kept low.

Plaiting schools slowly died out after the 1870 Education Act as this gave local School Boards the power to compel all children between 5 and 10 years to attend school. In the Toddington School log book is an 1872 entry: 'The Inspector of factories called twice at the school and enquired the names of the women in the town who kept plaiting schools. As a direct result several children from the plaiting schools were admitted as half-timers.'

The School Attendance Committee of the Woburn Union monitored parents who kept their children away from school. If the parents still declined to send their children to school they could be fined. On 22 October 1880 William Clarke, William Buckingham, John Marlow and Samuel Brown, all labourers of Toddington, were fined 5s each at the Petty Sessions for having disobeyed magisterial orders made upon them to send their children to school.

The village schools have been the heart of Toddington since 1854 and have provided a quality education for local children from Toddington and the surrounding district. Five schools have been used for education: The National School or Church of England School which later became the Voluntary Primary School, Station Road (1854-1967), The Wesleyan School, Leighton Road (1854-1910), The Council School in Leighton Road (1910-1963), Parkfields Secondary Modern (now Parkfields Middle School) which opened in 1963 and St George of England Primary School (now Toddington St George VC Lower School), opened in 1967.

The two elementary schools set up in 1854 were largely run on the 'monitorial' system. The headteacher instructed a few children, known as 'monitors' who then taught the other pupils. One teacher had the task of keeping a large school hall full of pupils in order, while the monitors who were pupils of about 14, tried by mechanical repetition to impart information to the children. The monitors asked set questions and the pupils would reply with the answer. If the questions were asked in the wrong order then the pupils would most likely give the wrong answer! Sand would be used by the younger pupils to make letters who then graduated to a slate and finally to a writing book. In 1862 the 'payment by results' system was started. Each child would be examined in the three R's- reading, writing and arithmetic by the inspectors. The number of passes determined the grant to the school and this in turn affected the teachers' salaries.

At first fees were charged for tuition. In 1865 the National School lowered the weekly fees from 2d to a 1d for labourers' children. In 1877 all children above the age of 7 were paying 3d each. It was not until 1891 that the fee was abolished and school became free.

In voluntary schools which were state-aided, religious teaching, appointment of staff, and the upkeep of buildings were the responsibility of the school managers. However the state had the right to inspect the teaching of non-religious subjects in order to ensure that the required standards were maintained.

The Education Act of 1902 set up Local Education Authorities under whose control all elementary education was vested. The school leaving age was gradually raised until in 1918 it was raised to 14. A distinction was made between junior and senior education.

The 1944 Education Act established a three stage continuous education process for all children between 5 and 18 years. The three stages were primary (5-11), Secondary 11-15 or 16) and Further Education. Children over 11 years were to receive a secondary education in either a modern, technical or grammar school according to their ability. The pupils had to be selected by a series of Intelligence Tests, a report from the primary school, by parents' wishes and by passing an entrance exam which became known as the 11-plus exam. If pupils did well at grammar school, a university education was available with fees paid and a maintenance allowance given.

The technical schools did not appear on the scale envisaged. It was thought at the time that the system would enable children to be educated according to their ability and preferences. Rather than educating children to their need or ability the 11-plus became seen as a question of passing or failing. This led to the exam being resented by some whilst others strongly supported the new system. The exam was formally abolished in England and Wales in 1976, giving way to the comprehensive system although some counties such as Buckinghamshire still retain some grammar schools.

When Kingsbury Grammar School in Dunstable opened in 1957 as a co-ed school it started with three year groups ie pupils who were 11, 12 or 13. In order to help fill the classrooms the brightest pupils aged 12 or 13 from Toddington County Secondary School were transferred to the new school. These pupils were given the chance of a grammar school education. Amongst those that transferrerd from Toddington to Kingsbury were: Frank Holman, Colin Bryson, Tom Shepherd, Richard Hancox, Robert Patterson, Pamela Wilson, Vilma Wilson, Paul Denton, Norman Buckman, Mary Tompkins, Michael Lane and Rita Sturgeon.

National School, Primary School and Lower School

In 1854 the National School in Station Road was opened. The school became possible through a bequest by William Dodge Cooper-Cooper and his wife. This consisted of a small plot of land containing '1 rood and 11 poles to the minister and churchwardens of Toddington in trust, for a school for the education of children and adults, or children only, of the labouring, manufacturing and other poorer classes in the parish'. The school was to be conducted according to the principles of the National Society. This meant that the minister could have the use of the premises on Sunday and the headteacher had to be a member of the Church of England. It was mainly controlled by the Church of England and the Manor. Although it was open to inspection and received a Government grant through the National Society for educating the poor, fees were charged.

The school, like the Wesleyan School which later became the Council School, offered an elementary education for pupils up to the age of 14 years. Bright children took exams and gained scholarship to Luton High School for girls and Luton Modern for boys.

The 1944 Education Act led to the schools being re-organised in 1947. The National School became Toddington Voluntary Primary School (Controlled). All costs were now met by the state. It now catered for pupils up to the age of 11 but was still affectionally referred to as the 'National School'.

The school needed more classrooms so in 1963, when Parkfields was opened, pupils between seven and eleven were sent to the classrooms in the vacant School in Leighton Road whilst the infants continued to be taught at Station Road. When the new school opened in Manor Road in 1967 all the pupils were transferred from Leighton Road and Station Road to the new school which was built on land next to Parkfields. The new school was called St George VC Primary School. Following a re-organisation of the schools in 1977 its name changed to St George VC Lower School, a lower school for pupils aged between five and nine.

The front of the Primary School in the 1960s. The house that the headteacher used to live in can be seen on the left. Mrs Wootton, the widow of the headteacher, lived there in the 1950s.

Wesleyan School, Council School and Parkfields

The Wesleyan Day School opened on 22 January 1855 'with upwards of sixty children'. Mr Marshall who trained at the Wesleyan Normal Institution, Westminster, was appointed 'master'. In 1909/10 a new school was built on adjacent land in Leighton Road and it then became known as the Council School with the Wesleyans losing some of their control and authority. Following the re-organisation in 1947 it became a Secondary Modern School, for children over the age of 11 years. In 1963 the school moved to a new site on part of the original Home Farm in Park Road and was renamed Parkfields. It served the children of Toddington and the surrounding villages of Chalton, Chalgrave, Eversholt, Harlington, Milton Bryan, Tebworth, Tingrith and Wingfield. Pupils could transfer at the age of sixteen to other secondary schools serving the area to follow courses leading to Advanced Level examinations. Further re-organisation took place in the 1970s with Parkfields becoming a middle school for children aged nine to twelve years, having its first 9+ year in 1977. Older children (13+) went to Harlington Upper School.

National School Pictures 1854–1915

The school opened in 1854 and fees were charged for tuition. In 1865 the school fees were lowered from 2d to a penny for labourers' children. The school was built to accommodate some 300 pupils.

The National School playground, about 1960. The windows were high up so that children could not see out. In 1910 it was recorded that: 'The stones in the playground do not seem much inclined to go in the ground. We borrowed a heavy roller today and in rolling the stones we broke the crank.' Richard Dillingham wrote in 1954: 'For years afterwards the state of the playground was a regular item on the agenda of managers. One eventually volunteered to make a house-to-house collection but apparently he did not meet with much success. Before 1952 there was only one wash basin between all the pupils and the toilets were at the back of the playground.'

The school was pulled down and six houses built on the land in 1970. Today part of the playground still remains as a car park.

Presentation- A quiet but very interesting ceremony took place in the National school-room, on Tuesday morning last. Miss Louisa Phillimore, whose term of apprenticeship as pupil teacher expires in a few days, having by her strict attention to duty, punctuality, and correct deportment generally gained the respect and esteem of the managers and friends of the school, it was determined to present a token of remembrance to her, previous to her departure for college. A subscription was set on foot and a beautiful walnut wood writing-desk purchased with the proceeds for the purpose. The rector, the Rev J. Clegg, who with his accustomed liberality, had contributed largely to the testimonial, was requested to present it. The rev. gentleman arrived punctually at the appointed time, and at once proceeded to business.

A Correspondent to the Beds Times, 1 December 1863.

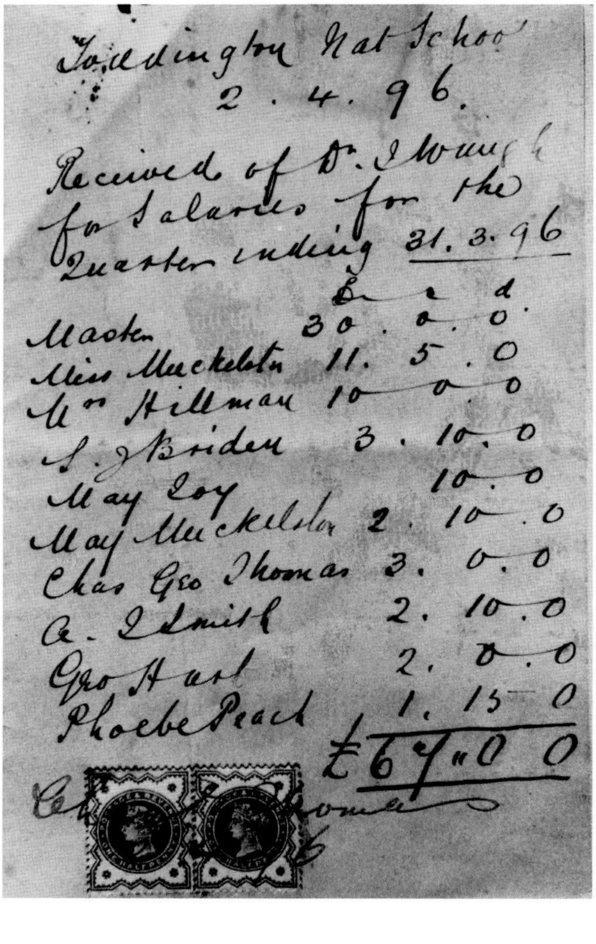

Toddington Nat School
2. 4. 96.
Received of Dr. J Waugh
for salaries for the
Quarter ending 31. 3. 96

	£	s	d
Master	30	0	0
Miss Mucklestn	11	5	0
Mrs Hillman	10	0	0
S. J Briden	3	10	0
May Loy		10	0
May Mucklestn	2	10	0
Chas Geo Thomas	3	0	0
A. E Smith	2	10	0
Geo Hart	2	0	0
Phoebe Peach	1	15	0
	£67	0	0

Chas Geo Thomas

Receipt from the headteacher Mr Thomas for the first quarter salaries of 1896 addressed to Dr Waugh, the village doctor. Phoebe Peach the school caretaker received £1 15s 0d or £1.75. Therefore her salary for the whole year would have been the princely sum of £7 compared with £120 for the headteacher. Phoebe was a previous pupil at the school. She was born on 25 January 1868 and was admitted to her first class at the age of three in February 1871. At the age of 10 she completed a sampler which is still on display. Samplers were pieces of embroidery produced to demonstrate or test needlework skill whilst learning letters of the alphabet and numerals.

This picture was taken in 1898. Pictured is Group V11 with May Addie née Evans sitting on a chair second from left.

Pupils had to call their teacher 'Miss' or 'Sir' and had to stand up to answer questions and wait for permission to speak. They also had to use their right hand at all times for writing. When an adult entered the classroom pupils were expected to stand. Transgressions were punished and these included swearing, kicking the teacher and spitting in girls' faces.

Because the school classes were so big, everything had to be done in a regimented way. The teacher would write things on the blackboard which were copied into books and learnt. A lot of teaching involved repetition. The names and dates of kings and queens and 'times' tables were learnt this way.

Teachers were often very strict and by modern standards very scary. A rap across the knuckles or a clip around the ears awaited anyone not doing what the teacher asked. The cane was also used.

Back row: H. Russell, B. Kent, A. Osborne, C. Randall, H. Sylvester. W. Muckleston.
4th row: H.Randall, C. Briden, B. Carr, W. Franklin, A. Beasley.
3rd row: L. Stedman. F. Fleckney, W. Seymour, G. Allen, - , Turvey, E. Whinnett, Mr Thomas.
2nd row: A. Kent, A. Barker, E. Warren, A. Ayres, A. Titmus, E. Thomas.
Front row: W. Horley, A. Hart, A. Carr.

Miss L. Horley's 1902 class.
Back row: C. Smith, R.S. Allen, Hollis, Chandler, Buckingham, S. Fletcher.
3rd row: P.Stiff, J. Wade, Brazier, B. Denton, H. Tearle, Reid, Goymer, Brewer.
2nd Row: S. Denton, K.Milbank, E. Bliss, L. Marlow, M. Dunham, Godfrey, E. Pearson (?)
Front Row: M. Sharpe, H. Teagles, E. Sharpe, L. Teagles, M. Evans, L. Brewer, V. Pateman.

Charles Euxine Thomas was headteacher from 1875-1914. He qualified at Battersea Training College. At the time of his appointment at the age of 21 he was single and his sister kept house for him. He lived rent free in a furnished house containing 'two chairs, a table and a bed'.

His death at the age of 60 was largely due to the heavy workload that he set himself. Weekdays started with his training of his pupil teachers from 8am to 8.45am. School was from 9 am to 12 noon and from 1.30 pm to 4 pm. On Saturdays he taught the pupil teachers from 9 am to 12 noon and the afternoons were occupied with various meetings. In the winter three nights were occupied with Night School. Sunday was taken up with Sunday School at 10 am, Church at 11am and Evensong at 6.30 pm. On alternate Sundays there was a Children's service. He was the church organist and choirmaster. While the girls were taught Plain Needlework and Cutting Out, Mr Thomas taught the boys drawing twice a week.

In 1878 Mr Thomas recorded: 'There are a great many fees in arrears, but we cannot press the payment of them too much, as many of the parents are out of work and have been for some time.' In the summer attendances were often thin because children were helping their parents in the fields. Unauthorised holidays were often taken to attend fetes and fairs.

He had high expectations of behaviour and appearance. For example Mr Thomas recorded: 'I caused a pail of water, a scrubbing brush, a flannel, some soap and a towel to be brought into the room and made some dirty boys wash themselves before the others.' On the day of his funeral all the shops closed and most of the private houses had their blinds drawn out of respect.

Sunday School Teachers Meeting- The teachers of St Georges' Church Sunday Schools held an important meeting at the Rectory on Friday evening last. It was decided that during the winter months the smaller children should have service in the Sunday School in the morning, during the time of Divine service at the church, and thus be kept in the warm, instead of marching from school in the cold to attend service at the church.

Luton News, 6 October 1892.

Recalling days of hoops and tops,
When, on the way to school, you'd go
And buy a bag of lollipops
Or butterscotch, from Jennie Rowe.
Or, on the green, would stay leap-frogging
Until the stroke of nine would send
You , and your fellow scholars, jogging
Up Leighton road, down Tanner's End.

When from "Fox Hunts" through copse and tarn
You'd scramble home all shreds and patches,
When football "fans" thronged Alma Farm,
And Hobbs's Close meant cricket matches.

Extract from a poem entitled Old Boys
by William Hyde

School Class, 1900. Pictured are:
Back row V. Harlow, J. Nash, F. Ireland, G. Rowe, B. Russell, T. Clarke, S. Millbank.
3rd row: C. Anderson, A. Seymour, - , F. Everitt, W. George, H. Thomas.
2nd row: -, Allen, I. Kingham, H. Shepherd, -, Flecknal, B. Fowler, B. Randall.
Front row: Shepherd, F. Brazier, T. Shaw, H. Potts, M. Marlow, E .Denton.
Headteacher: C. E. Thomas.

Class 1902, with teachers Annie Walker (left) and Flora Clark (right). Learning to write began in the infants. Slates were used with a pencil made of clay. The accepted way of cleaning the slate was to spit on it and then wipe it with your sleeve. Annie Walker used to take the five year olds. However she did take some of the older girls for needlework. The older boys did woodwork and used to walk to the Council School where they shared the facilities. The boys also took part in Physical Exercise and Military Drill.

The National School- The distribution of prizes took place at the National School on Friday afternoon, by the Rev F.A. Adams. Books to the number of 131 were distributed among the infants, and in the mixed department prizes were given to each child, who made 400 attendances out of a possible 430. Fifty-four boys and fifty-four girls obtained the awards. In addition to the attendance prizes in each standard, merit prizes were given; these were for punctuality, cleanliness, attention, and progress. In Standard 1, nine prizes were given, Margaret Thomas being first; and in standards 11 to V11, the first prizes were awarded respectively to Wilfred Joy, Harry Timms, Horace Briden, Emily Timms, Charles Thomas and Sarah J. Briden. The latter also received a very handsome writing case for acting as sewing monitor. The pupil teachers and assistants likewise received small gifts.

Luton News, 12 May 1892.

In Victorian and Edwardian times girls wore dark coloured dresses protected by a white apron. These clothes were often hand-me downs. Compare the 'uniform' the girls are wearing on the opposite page to the two 1960s uniforms shown here.

Class 1902, with teacher Miss E. Smith. Pictured are pupils: R. Clifford, E. Coles, P. Denton, Potts, B. Cox, F. Kingham, C. Allen, H. Brown, W. Marlow, J. Coles, W. Peach, A. Falberg, F. George, A. Gazeley, F. Bates, S. Evans, E. Cousins, M. Gordon, F .Read, A. Kingham, H. Evans, J. Washington, F. Larkin, G. Garner, M. Shaw, W. Ansell, L. Clarke (not all names are listed).

George Parien Hart is the teacher with this 1902 class.
Back row: A Gordon, C. Allen, - , J. Muckleston, - , - .
3rd row: M. Peake, C. Titmus, C. Muckleston, Hart, W.Williams, D Randall.
2nd row: M. Smith, L. Chandler, E.Carr, L. Buckingham, M.George, Seymour, D. Fane.
Front row: A. Sharpe, K. Frost, A. Ayres, R. Russell, J. Walters.

Ms Blower's 1902 Class. Back row: W. Neale, - , B. Ireland, Hart, M. Fane, J. Gordon, Bright, - . The windowsills of the school were high up so there were no distractions. The school at this time had a Savings Bank but no library.

Dr W. G. Grace, England's most famous batsman, pictured in 1904 at Toddington Park. He dominated cricket for decades, both for England and as captain of Gloucestershire. In 1895 he became the first batsman to reach 100 centuries in first-class cricket .

He visited the Park on several occasions. The cricket pitch was in the grounds of this large house on the way to Milton Bryan. On the 14 and 15 September 1899 it was recorded in the school log book: 'School dismissed at 2.55pm as Dr Grace, his son, Lockwood and several other professional cricketers are playing a two days' match at the Park. The children together with many of the onlookers were entertained by their host, Mr R.S. Sievier, to tea.'

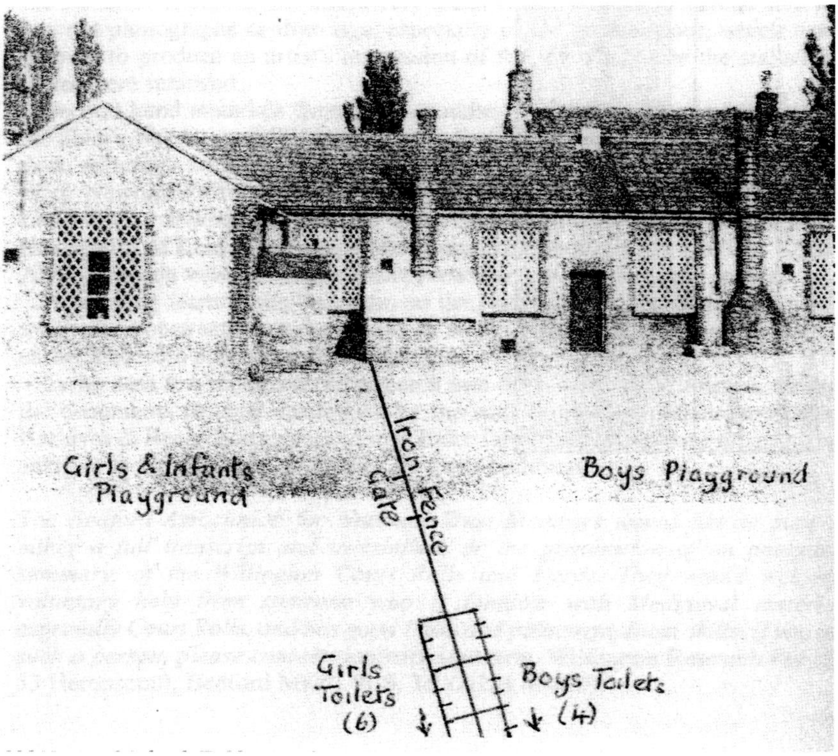

An iron fence with a gate divided the playground into two. The boys were on one side and girls and infants on the other. The toilets consisted of wooden sheds with buckets and were situated 'back to back' on either side of the fence. Toilet paper as such was unknown. Instead newspaper cut into squares attached to string sufficed. There was an additional urinal for the boys at the end of the playground. In 1952 proper toilets were installed and Fred Bonner, one of the school managers remarked that 'it was the best thing that had ever happened in Toddington'.

'I remember the coalman stopping near the school with his horse and cart. The horse decided to relieve himself in the road and I followed his example. I did a wee at the side of the horse and Mrs Wootton saw me out of her room and told Mr Wootton the headmaster. I got into trouble over it. He told me off. My dad gave me a clout when I got home.

I went to the National school until I was 11 then I went to Luton Modern School. I think there were four of us who used to go. We used to go by train as there were no buses. We biked to Harlington to catch the train to Luton. Then holiday times we used to walk home from Luton. When we broke up we always seemed to break up at dinner time - 12 o'clock - no train, so we used to walk home and get home before 2pm. There was a train at 2 o'clock but we never used to bother to wait for it. We used to pay about 6d per week and leave our bikes at Harlington. The house on the corner near the station had a yard. You could leave it where the car park is now but you had to pay more money. I think the boys were Reg Cleaver, Ron Briden, Fred Bonner who lived along the Bridleway and me. There was also Marjory Gray and Freda Ayres. A little bit later Mary Mountfort and some others came. It was an all boy's school in Park Square. The Girls School was in a residential area.'

Ron Mountfort, born 1916.

Taken in October 1915 when unqualified teachers like Ella Neale (standing right) were paid £50 per annum.
Back Row: B. Clifford, G. Ashby, G. George, F. Sharp, H. Thompson, J. Pateman, F. Childs, J. Whitbread.
Middle Row: N. Buckingham, C. Atkinson, Master Sutton, A. Smith, N. Smith, A. Dodson, M. Walters, L. Smith.
Front Row: M. Randall, M Jarvis, A. Babister, F. Fountain, N. Groom, L. Smith, J. Buckingham, A. Wright.

1915 Class: Back row: Ernie Evans, Tom Smith, Reg Buckingham?, Hubert Groom, Reg Buckingham? Frank Brown. Middle row: Will Pratt, Will Joy, Olive Bennett Minnie Dodson, Minnie Wright, Alice Brewer, Blance Dennis, Tom Dennis, Gilbert Wood, Rupert Wood. Front row: Tom George, Mollie Walters, Nancy Walker, Edith Stanton, Doris Potts, Violet Whitbread, Sylvia Shelton, Tom Gadsden.

Conger House where Col Fawcett and his family lived.

These memories of Miss Patricia Fawcett born 24 March 1915 are composed from an interview given in 1982 to the Toddington Historical Society. She was the daughter of Colonel Fawcett, who was Toddington's doctor from his arrival just after the First World War until his death in 1951.

'My brother Llewellyn (known as "Lou") at first shared a governess with me, and at some point went to a private school at Battlesden, near Woburn. I don't believe he ever boarded - he was so delicate, with asthma. Later he had a tutor at Bedford. After my brother went to school, I shared a governess with the little girl at the Manor. One term she used to come to me, and another I went to her, in the pony and trap. Another time I shared a governess with a girl at Harlington Manor, but I didn't like her very much. We didn't get on very well. Our governess lived in our house. We had several - and some got the sack for smacking me. I wasn't used to such treatment, although I probably deserved it. I was taught Reading, History, Geography, copybook writing - I liked that, there was no brainwork attached; and I must have done Mathematics, I suppose! When I was twelve I went as a boarder to Heronsfield School at Chorleywood. It was run by two sisters of the wife of the vicar of Harlington - she and the vicar were friends of ours. I was there about three years. I then went as a private boarder to Crescent House School at Bedford.'

Toddington Manor

School Days in the 1920s

The following is a recording of a conversation with the late Mary Mountfort née Ireland who started school in 1924:

'There were two schools, the National School and the Council School. Church of England children went to the National School, and Chapel and other children went to the Council School. The headteacher of the National School used to be a Church person. In my day Mr Wootton was the headmaster and he was also the choirmaster. You went to whichever school your parents wanted you to go to. You did not have to put your name down like you do nowadays for a school. There was quite a rivalry between the two schools. The National School used to get better results than the Council School.

I started at the age of 5 and used to walk to school from Fancott. Dad used to have a milk round and if he was on time I used to have a ride with him. However more times than not I had to walk. I used to take sandwiches for dinner as there were no school lunches. Sometimes the headmaster, Mr Wootton, would bring us a hot drink and we would sit in the schoolroom by the open fire. In fact when it was very cold weather the pupils at the front of the class got warm and they would rotate with those at the back so that everyone had a chance of getting warm. Mrs Hobbs was the caretaker and the older boys from the top class used to get the coal for the fire. During playtime they used to shut the smaller pupils in the coal shed and hold the door shut. The classrooms were quite big.

Inkwell monitors used to keep the inkwells full. We used plasticine boards and slates and chalk. When I was 5 and in the 5-7 year class we were given silly things to do. We sat at long desks and were given material to pull to bits. "What do we want to do that for?" I asked. The teacher said: "You are a rude little girl. I shall see your mother". I replied "I think it is a waste of time". It was supposed to be good for your fingers.

Miss Higgs took sewing and we used to sew pillowcases that could be sold. They were sold to get money to buy more material. I was given a special one to do. I pricked my finger and blood went on the pillowcase. I was so upset. I went home and cried and my Mum said "Whatever is the matter" and I said "I pricked my finger and blood went on the pillowcase and they cannot sell it now". Mum replied: "Don't worry, I'll give you the money and you take it and we will have it. We will soon get the blood out."

Because I was bright I was put into Mr Wootton's class to get my scholarship for Luton High School. The brighter pupils were two years younger than the rest of the class. The older children in the class used to do cookery or woodwork. They used to do woodwork at the Leighton Road School as there was a special hut there. The brighter pupils were left on their own. A curtain divided the big schoolroom (later a partition). Well one of the boys that was left he got a pea shooter and shot through the gap in the curtain. As the peas landed Miss Higgs the teacher kept saying "What was that?" "What was that?" Well I was laughing. All those sort of things you could get away with then.

Mr Wootton used to slap your wrists. Miss Higgs used to make a great performance of it. If you were wearing a blouse she used to make you unbutton your sleeves before hitting your wrists.

Miss Ashcroft who later married and became Mrs Joy just used to give you a look and that was that. I never saw the cane being used. The parents never complained about their child being smacked. Sometimes the child would get another smack from their parents for being naughty.

You took the scholarship at 11 years. There was one test about March in the National School that Mr Wootton did. If you did well in that you went to school in Luton to take their entrance exam. Then if you were accepted you went to the school in the following September and did not leave until you were 16. I stayed on until I was 18 as I wanted to teach. It was a girl's school where you had to wear your hat at the right angle, a gym slip at the right length and you were not allowed to walk in threes only twos. You were not supposed to talk on the bus. Some children paid to go to the High School. They had to pass a certain exam so not everyone could go. If they passed and their parents had the money they were allowed to go.

If you did not pass the scholarship you stayed at the National School until you were 14 and then left to do apprenticeships or work in shops.

We used to have a free pass to go on the bus and every term when we had a report it had to go to Shire Hall Bedford for the Director of Education to see. He would sign his name at the top in red. One term I decided not to work as hard as I had done- I decided to have a rest. I did not get a very good report and my Mum made me take the report to Mr Wootton. He said I needed to get on with it otherwise I would not get my free bus pass and then you will be finished. Do not let this happen again was underlined in red. It was not a happy atmosphere like it is today with youngsters.

Next to the Fancott Arms lived the Bowers family-there were quite a few of them- George, Henry, Billy, Frank, Florie, Henry and John. Then there was Bob (same age as Fred Ireland) and Madge Carr, Bob Marlow, George (died of diphtheria), Reg Marlow and Sally Kingham. Sally lived with her grandparents who kept ducks. They lived at the cottage opposite the Marlows *(White Hart Farm)*. Sally knew her mother but not her father. Her father had gone for a soldier-meaning she was illegitimate- a stigma in those days. There were also Fred Bonner and Irene Bonner who lived along the Bridleway. With all these playmates I used to play cricket, hide and seek, hoops (played in the road), and hop scotch. We used to congregate at the end of the lane. When we were at school we would say "are you coming out tonight" and Mum would say you could go for half-an-hour and no more. If we didn't come home on time we were not allowed out the next day. Homework was quite hard and I used to stick at it and go out when I had finished. There was no electricity –we had candles and paraffin lamps. I used to do my homework on the kitchen table with the paraffin lamp while the rest of the family talked. There was no question of me finding a quiet spot in the front room the fire was lit only on Sundays. In this room was a piano on which I practised by candlelight.

I applied to Avery Hill College in Eltham London to train as a teacher. Well my Mum nearly had a fit when I told her I had to go to London for an interview because she had never been to London. She found a friend to go with me to London for the interview. I got into Avery Hill and stayed there for two years before getting a teaching post in St Albans. We went out better trained than some of them today even though it was two years and not the three years that it later became. Today they do not stick to the three Rs enough. I stayed at the St Albans school until I got married. When Miss Walker retired, she took the reception, Mr Wootton rang me up to say would I like her job so I said "Yes" as I had to bike to Leagrave and then get the train. It was alright when I was living at Fancott but when I was living in Toddington it made it a long day. Anyway Miss Walker would not hand in her resignation. I was not going to hand mine in until she had resigned. Mr Wootton worked on her. Both St Albans and Toddington were Church of England schools.

I did not work in Toddington after teaching college because people would know me by my Christian name. Well the first morning at Toddington School there was one little beggar, Andy Palmer was his name. He used to see me on Sundays delivering the milk and called me Mary. "Hello Mary" he said as he came into the playground. I took him to one side and said: "You can call me Mary on Sundays but at school you call me Mrs Mountfort". I stayed at the school until I was expecting Mary E and then Kate came along. I helped Ron in the shop for a bit. They were short of a teacher in the reception class and Mr Dillingham rang up. I went back when Kate was 6 years old.'

Mary Mountfort retires in 1979 after 23 years at St George's Lower School. Headmaster, Norman Lymbery, presents Mary with a radio, a cheque for £70 and an ornament. Retired teacher Mrs Joy (left) looks on.

Class 1925:
Back Row: R. Stringer, F. Jellis, E. Evans, - , Hymus, - , E. Bonner, - , C. Cole, - , W. Shepherd.
Fourth Row: Miss Higgs, M. Gray, E. Muckleston, M. Gadsden, L. Evans, M. Bates, J. Fox, A. Simmonds, M. Hucklesby, E. Buckingham.
Third row: A. Smith, F. Ayres, E. Bland, - , -, Atkinson, - , H. Bowers, R. Brown, H.Smith, F. Ireland, A. Brewer, H. Ansell, - .
Second row: E. Smith, E. Bland, M.Gordon, E.Bolter, P. Kingham.
Front row: C. Gordon, F. Peddar, - , - , Buckingham, R. Athews. F. Sturgeon,

A group of pupils and headteacher Mr B.M. Wootton display the Madeline Hyde Shield which they won at the Toddington and District Children's Day, 1925.

School Days in the 1930s

Priscilla Hart née Ireland gives her account:

'I started at the National School in Station Road in 1930 and at the age of five years, could write my name, knew the alphabet and knew my numbers, and lots of rhymes. This was thanks to my eldest sister Mary, who at a very early age knew she wanted to be a teacher, and it was her pleasure to line up all our dolls and teddies, plus me and pretend to be teaching! I certainly had to do as I was told - a good training for school life.

My first teacher at school was Miss Annie Walker, and I can still remember clearly the wooden frame on a stand at the front of the class on which we learnt to weave by passing a stick through the bands of braid. The next class was taken by Miss Dolemore (Mrs Pett). Here, I remember copying letters of the alphabet in pencil and the joy of receiving a present from Father Christmas after the school play - it was a table tennis set. Next came Miss Flora Seymour, (Mrs Nelsey) and here there was a great competition to get your sums right. Every Friday afternoon, she produced a sweet tin and each pupil that had done well chose his or her favourite humbug. Miss Garratt (Mrs Briden) later took over the class and then followed Miss Elizabeth Higgs, famous for her history lessons. My final teacher was Miss Ashcroft (Mrs Joy). In this class, Miss Ashcroft really made us work every year. Some pupils passed the external exams for the High (girls), the Modern (boys) and Technical (mixed) schools in Luton. She was excellent with a sewing needle and taught us girls to hem, darn and embroider. Hard words to spell were remembered by rhymes or song, e.g., Mrs D, Mrs I, Mrs F.F.I., Mrs C, Mrs U, Mrs L.T.Y. - difficulty. On Friday afternoons we had the treat of a story, when she read about *The Christmas Carol, Kidnapped* and *Water Babies* etc. Many a tear was shed and a smile made as her voice altered for each character, to make the books come alive.

Mr Bruce Wootton was headteacher and taught the eldest pupils. He was good with handling unruly boys, and was keen on music and gardening. A curtain divided his class from Miss Higg's, and many a time a splash of ink was thrown from an ink pen onto this curtain, hoping to hit a pupil in the lower class. Inkwells were filled up each morning by pupils and also coke brought into school from the coal shed for the school stoves.

As I lived a mile away from school, I was allowed to stay to school lunch. These were cooked and served on the premises of the Council School in Leighton Road, and eaten in the School Hall. The chief cook was Mrs Crawley, and later Mrs Crump, and they will long be remembered for their spotted dicks and treacle puddings with custard. Every girl having a dinner took turns in helping to prepare the vegetables and wash up afterwards. A few lessons were missed in the peeling of potatoes etc. and time lost in the dinner hour with washing up - the boys were not expected to do these chores!

In the early 1930s I used to bus to school in winter (1d fare from Fancott Bridleway near the letter box to Toddington Green), and walk on the fine summer days. In the spring we used to count the number of dead frogs lying in the road from Fancott clay pits to the hill - sometimes it came to over 100. They had all been run over and squashed flat! Another game was to walk the first two telegraph poles, and then run the next. As I grew older and owned my first bicycle, this was a great way of travelling. Also when I received a pair of roller skates, these were used for skating the mile to school and then used in the playground as well, especially when roller skates were the "in" game. Everything had its seasons - skipping (a large long rope was great fun). Ball playing, singing games like *The Big Ship Sails through the Alley Alley O.* Whips and Tops - I still have two wooden tops from those days, they are well worn at the pointed stud end, and still have traces of the coloured chalk patterns on their tops. What a tale they could tell! Another game was the Oxford and Cambridge Favours, which we children could buy in the local shops very cheaply. Light blue for Cambridge, dark blue for Oxford. The favour of the team you chose was pinned on your dress or coat, and then you would try and convert others to your side. I used to buy mine (Cambridge) from Mr Harry Timms who had a grocery sweet shop in Station Road (opposite the Baptist Chapel). These favours used to hang on a card just outside the shop, to catch the eye of children passing by. He also sold sherbet dabs, gobstoppers, aniseed balls and licorice comforts, to name but a few of the favourite sweets for children.

School sports were held in Mr Ayres' field next to the school playground. We were allocated into four Houses as Teams - Red, Yellow, Green and Blue. I remember great excitement one day when Johnny Kempton (younger brother to W.M. Kempton, who ran the cycle business in the High Street in later years) jumped higher than himself. Extra holidays were always enjoyed - especially Pancake Day (Shrove Tuesday) when the older children were allowed out of school at 11:50am to run over to Conger Hill and when the pancake bell tolled at midday, listen to the old woman frying her pancakes. We really believed we could hear the sizzling. Empire Day (24 May) and Ascension Day were also half-day holidays. With the latter it was a service in church and then the older children were allowed to go up the church tower.

For various reasons, some children would not attend school. Mr Cross, the education attendance officer, would often appear on parents' doorsteps to know the reason why; in fact his name only had to be mentioned in Toddington and some parents and pupils would tremble - such was the fear of the man!

The school dentist used to visit schools about once a year and he and his nurse used to take over a small classroom for his visit. Of course none of us liked his treatment and another dislike was the nurse who looked in your hair for nits.

When I was old enough to cycle on my own, I was asked by my parents to check the flock of sheep we had in pastures rented down Long Lane (we always called it Tingrith Lane). This was often done after school lunch, quite a ride in the summer months to Hobbins Green Field, halfway down the Lane. The number of sheep were counted, checked that none lay on their backs, and also that they were free from maggot fly.

These are happy years to look back on and I am sure many other children who grow up in Toddington during the 1930s will agree that although some of us were poor in wealth we were blessed with good parents, had the company of loving brothers and sisters and good friends. Toddington was indeed a special place in which to grow up.'

Beryl Hyde née Evans concludes with recollections of her schooldays in the 1930s:

'I was marched off to school, aged four and three quarters into Miss Annie Walker's class. Annie, who lived at No. 30 Market Square, the tiny cottage on the Green taught the infant class at the National School for 47 years. On my first day she produced a photograph of my father, taken when he was in her class, aged three and a half, with his dummy pinned on his jersey.

In the corner in front of the class was a large doll's house, which I thought was wonderful. At the end of the term some of us were allowed to take home an item for washing and I was given the covers from the bed. I couldn't wait to get home with them. Although most children loved Annie she could be very strict and when I was asked one day if I was ever smacked by her I replied, "No, but she gives you a jolly good poke".

At the age of eight I was in the class of Miss Elizabeth Higgs, who came from a well known family in Westoning. She would get very irate if we talked or misbehaved and I remember her hitting one boy so hard on his legs with her ruler that the ruler broke in two. We kids would chant, not in her hearing of course, "Lizzie's got the rats up!"

Mr. Wootton, a very respectful gentleman, had been headteacher since 1914, having first joined the school in 1912 as an assistant master. He was also choirmaster at St. George's Church and much loved by staff and pupils alike.

Mrs Annie Hobbs, the wife of Nag Hobbs was the school caretaker. Affectionately known as Black Annie, she was a lady almost as wide as she was high and not always the cleanest of bodies, hence her nickname, but she remained caretaker for 37 years.

The largest room in the school, which also served as a hall, was divided into two by a large white curtain edged in red and with the shield of St. George appliquéd on. In one half Mr. Wootton taught the top class of children who were coming up to the leaving age of 14 while in the other half, sitting at old fashioned long desks, were two more classes. Learning became a little difficult when the top class behind the curtain had a singing lesson and renderings of *Where the Bee Sucks* and *Nymphs and Shepherds* competed with a history lesson and the Battle of Hastings!

The old tortoise stove at one end of the large room had to be made up twice a day by the older boys and the smell of it met you as you walked in. There was no free milk but for tuppence halfpenny a week we could have hot Horlicks in the morning playtime and the container would sit on top of the stove, keeping warm. A great favourite of mine were the Horlicks Malted Milk tablets costing a halfpenny for eight that we could also buy.

Mention must be made of the school toilets which seem almost unbelievable today as we aren't talking of the 17th Century but the 1930s! They were placed up the centre of the playground – long before mains water – boys on one side and girls on the other. They had doors with a small gap at the top and a large gap at the bottom so, if you recognised the shoes and socks, you knew who was in there. There were no locks on the doors so we girls were terrified when the rough element of boys came along kicking the doors, hoping they would fly open and reveal all. You certainly didn't stay in there any longer than was necessary, for more reasons than one. The only means of washing your hands was an enamel bowl on a stand in the playground. Every now and then we would have a Clean Hands Campaign. We were each given a special card and if you had signed it for a whole month to prove that you had washed your hands before and after every meal, you received a badge picturing two hands.

On Shrove Tuesday, as our parents and grandparents had done before us, we all went up and piled on top of Conger Hill.

At precisely twelve o'clock the pancake bell would ring and we'd put our ears to the ground and definitely hear the old woman frying her pancakes. On Ascension Day, we were marched to church in the morning. The top class were allowed to climb up the tower and then we were all given a half day holiday. On Empire Day (that was when we had an Empire) we would march round the playground saluting the Union Flag. On the day of the University Boat Race, the school was divided between Oxford and Cambridge and the appropriate colour rosette of either dark or light blue worn, according to which crew you supported. Sports Day was another happy event in the school year and was held in Mr Allen's field, where Chapel Close is today.

Two favourite stopping off places on the way home from school were the pump and the pond as they both had railings for swinging on and performing our gymnastics. In those days the pond was much larger than it is today and came up to where the slip road is now. It was quite shallow at the front and in the summer we would paddle and then play on the railings until our feet dried. In the winter when it was frozen over we'd make long slides and slide down them, with hands round each other's waist.

The picture of ducks on the pond today is not a new one; there were plenty of them there then.

After the Second World War the pond was reduced in size and made into the beautiful Memorial Gardens we see today, dedicated to all those parishioners who gave their lives during the World Wars.

There used to be a cluster of cottages by the pond and what a village scene of a by-gone age they created. Some very poor families lived there including two families of gypsies. One was called Smith and the other Ellis, and the two girls, Comfort and Lavinia Ellis attended school with us. There was no mistaking them with their starched pinafores and their hair scragged back in plaits, looking as though they had been scrubbed with carbolic soap. I also remember a gypsy boy called Johnny Smith.'

Teachers, 1930s. Pictured:
Back row: Mr Wootton, Miss Ashcroft (Mrs Joy).
Front row: Flora Seymour (Mrs Nelsey), Miss Higgs, Miss Dolemore (Mrs Pett).

Miss Walker and Miss Ashcroft, 1929.

Miss Ashcroft (later Mrs Joy) lodged with Mrs Horley at The Chestnuts in Dunstable Road. When she got married she went to live with her husband Billy in Leighton Road. It was quite common for teachers to live in lodgings until they got married.

Mrs Joy taught several generations of children. One of her former pupils stated: 'She was lovely and used to read The Wind in the Willows *to us every afternoon'. She used to cycle around the village on an old bike with a basket on the front.*

Edie Marlow went to Chalton school until the age of 11 and then transferred to the National School where she left at 14 to work in Luton as a hat trimmer. She was taught needlework by Miss Walker. Eric Caldecourt was paid 1d by Miss Walker for fetching water from the village pump to her cottage on the green. He recalls that 'she was a real old spinster who laid the law down'.

Children's Day, about 1930 in the recreation ground. It began in 1924 and was the brain child of James Hyde. There were various competions which included poetry, drawing, needlework, painting and essay writing. Almost every child entered the fancy dress competion.

School playground, 1930s. Mr Wootton can be seen supervising playtime. One time Mr Wootton fell over in the playground and broke his ankle. All the children laughed! Miss Ashcroft took over and she was very strict.

The playground was divided in two by iron railings to separate the juniors from the seniors. The railings went during the Second World War. The toilets were at the back of the playground and consisted of buckets which were emptied once a week by the Friday night cart. In the 1940s the boys used to have a competition to see who could wee over the corrugated sheet that formed part of the outside toilets. There was only one wash basin between the whole school.

The children are wearing their school colours in their lapels. Miss Annie Walker and Miss Higgs looked after the juniors whilst Mr Wootton supervised the seniors. Before coming into school the boys would rush over to Tanners End Farm, which was opposite the school, at the time of cutting the corn, to kill rats and mice, and on occasion carry a mouse into school.

Class 1930, pictured in the school house garden.
Back row: A. Gray, R.Cossons, S. Smith, B.Atkinson, B. Hyde, G. Hucklesby, D. Paterson.
Third row: I. Dyer, S. Smith, S. Kingham, L. Neal, S .Brewer, Z. Innel, M. Ireland, N .Brown, M. Hyde.
Second row: P. Blackman, M. Randall, V. Smith, M. Timms, V. Buckingham, M. George, Ayres, N. Paterson.
Front row: H. Briden, E. Atkinson, R. Marlow, W. Denton, J. Kempton, B. Gordon.

In those days to call out in class was a grave offence. If you wanted to say something you had to put your hand up.

National School Class, 1930.

Standing: Fred Buckingham, May Brewer, Mary Randall, Bertie Atkinson, Winnie Fowler, Aubrey Gray, Leslie Brazier, Teddy Janes, Mary Ireland, Winnie Wand.
Sitting: Sylvia Smith, Laura Ansell, Zero Innell, Sarah Brewer, Ivy Dyer, George Hucklesby, Dan Paterson, Gladys Kingham, Albert Gordon.

Teachers used to give out sweets at the end of the week to the pupils who had done well with their times tables.

Picture taken in 1930 of school pupils with the Madeline Hyde Shield won at Sports Day between the National School and the Council School. Pictured are: Back row: Mr Wootton, Bob Aldred, Horace Briden, Dan Briden, Les Brazier, Bob Marlow, Fred Ireland, Howard Ansell, Bill Shepherd.
Middle row: Zoe Innel, Lily Neal , Sarah Brewer, Laura Ansell, Marjorie Timms, Marjorie Grange.
Front Row: Annie Brewer, Joan Randall, Dora Clark , Violet Stapleton, Dorothy Odell, Joan Fox, Winnie Ward, Mary Ireland.

School Athletic Team, 1935. Back row: G. Griffiths, J. Gordon, Mr B.M Wootton.
Front row: J. Muckleston, E. Clifford, M. Janes, D. Hyde. The team are displaying the Madeline Hyde Shield which they won at Toddington and District Children's Day which was held in the recreation ground in Luton Road. It was started in 1924 by James Hyde and was held on every Whit Monday. There was great rivalry between the schools when it came to the sporting events. The Children's Day Challenge Shield was given in memory of Madeline Joy Hyde who died on 11 February 1925 aged 3 years.

National School House Sports and Netball Competition, July 1932, held in Mr Allen's field where Chapel Close is now. The buildings behind are in Leighton Road. The winning house received the Toddington Church of England House Cup.

Out of school the children played hopscotch, skipping and rounders. They also liked bowling a hoop or whipping a spinning top in the road. These hoops were made of wood or steel, the boys loving the steel ones for the noise they made.

Tug-of-War in progress, 1935. Tug-of-war had a higher status within athletics during the first half of the 20th century. It was represented by teams in every summer Olympics from 1900 to 1920. The schoolchildren did not have the benefit of the gym so PE normally took place in the playground. The school like many elementary schools had no games fields and the pupils never got the chance of a proper games lesson.

Bruce Wootton, headteacher 1914-50. David Morgan gives the following account:

'It was my privilege to know Mr Wootton, albeit for but a few months. He'd come to Toddington as a qualified assistant teacher in 1912 but took over as headteacher when his predecessor retired. Much was expected of the 'heads' of Church Schools between the wars. They were expected to set a good example all round; to be the rector's right-hand man; to be in charge of the Boy Scouts; raise funds to maintain the fabric of the building and pay for teaching materials. And last, but certainly not least, to raise money towards his own salary. Mr Wootton did all this and more. He was village correspondent for the Luton News *and the Sun Insurance Company. During the Second World War he was the Citizens' Advice Bureau. He never grumbled about his load but I am in no doubt the effort, over such a long period, shortened his life.*

He died in harness, months before he was due to retire. He ran a happy school and was greatly respected by both staff and pupils; and his relationship with the head of the Secondary Modern, Mr Young, was excellent. I was once loaned to him to help with his last Sports Day. I shall never forget it, it was a complete romp much enjoyed by everyone and not a stopwatch in sight.'

Mr Wootton died at his home, *The School House*, Toddington, aged 60. Mr Wootton, who was well known for his many local activities was headmaster of Toddington Church School for over 35 years, and had been choirmaster of Toddington Parish Church since 1914. He was also a member of the Parish Council and the Toddington Almshouse Charities and hon. secretary of the Parochial Church Council.

He had been Scoutmaster at Toddington and for many years Sunday School Superintendant. Mr Wootton served in both wars, in the last war being an air raid warden, billeting officer and food officer. He had also been chairman of the local Conservative Association and a member of the British Legion. He was for many years Toddington correspondent for the the *Luton News*.

Luton News, 1950.

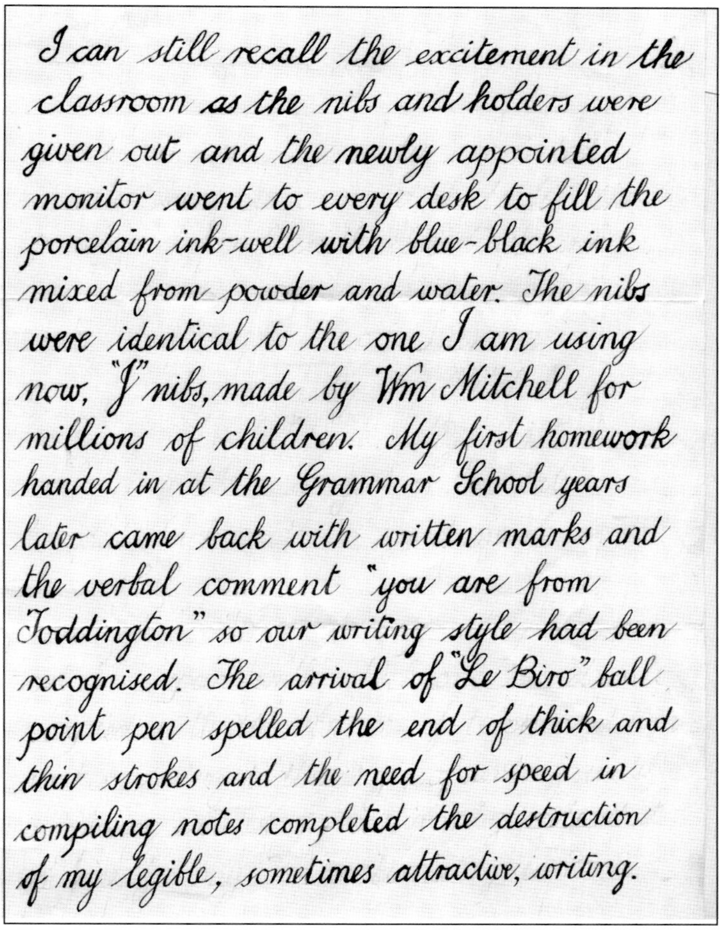

I can still recall the excitement in the classroom as the nibs and holders were given out and the newly appointed monitor went to every desk to fill the porcelain ink-well with blue-black ink mixed from powder and water. The nibs were identical to the one I am using now, "J" nibs, made by Wm Mitchell for millions of children. My first homework handed in at the Grammar School years later came back with written marks and the verbal comment "you are from Toddington" so our writing style had been recognised. The arrival of "Le Biro" ball point pen spelled the end of thick and thin strokes and the need for speed in compiling notes completed the destruction of my legible, sometimes attractive, writing.

Eric Caldecourt arrived in Toddington in September 1939, having been evacuated with his family from Clerkenwell in London on the day war broke out.

'We were taken in, befriended and housed by the Hyde and Ireland families; my friendship with the last of that generation continues to this day.

I started school in London aged 4 at a rather unusual establishment called Hugh Middleton School in Clerkenwell – he was some kind of financial benefactor whose ideas on education were miles in front of the times. Having had two years at this school I could already read, write and do simple arithmetic but as a "new kid" I was put in with my sister in Miss Walker's infant class. After half a morning she took me (by the ear) and passed me this time to Mrs Sadler, where I managed to stay a little longer but before Christmas she passed me on to Miss Higgs who had the 8/9 year olds as I recall it. She also had a bookcase full of exciting books which we were encouraged to read – and I did , and still do read avidly. While with Miss Higgs she must have pointed out to Mr Wootton that I liked singing. Hence my invite into the church choir where I remained for about six years – to the time my voice broke.

The infants class still used 'slate boards' and chalk. The A4 size slate was framed in a narrow wooden boarder. Together with the slate was a rag to wipe it clean, though who cleared up the chalk mess I do not know.

From Miss Higgs I moved up eventually to Miss Ashcroft (later Mrs Joy), where I stayed until I passed the entrance exam to the grammar school in 1944. I have many happy memories of her and the books she read us. With the correct pen and some time to spare I can still do the copperplate lettering she taught us.'

School 1946/7

Back Row
Rev Hunt
Mr B. Wootton (Head)
Miss Higgs
—
Miss Ashcroft
(Mrs Joy)

Eigth Row
—
Pamela Oliver
Margaret Kingham
Marjorie Brinklow
Winnie Underwood
Betty Muckleston
Pearl Muckleston
Janice Skeer?
Kathleen Pett
Betty Fossitt
Irene Hucklesby
—
Joy Baker
—
Harry Cook
Richard Cooke?
Jeffrey Dennis
—
—
—
Peter Gordon
—
Derek Bryant
Peter Jellis?
Derek Gordon

Seventh Row
Ethel Ray
Ann Molyneaux
Nellie Roberts
Maragret Payne
Laura Irving
Gloria Palmer
Ann Morgan
Jennifer Cooke
Valerie Pateman
Verna Muckleston
—
Maisie Hucklesby
Maisie Bullen
Sheila Payne
Pat Holmes
Pat Childs
Eileen Greengrass
Barabara Caldecourt
Vera Prince
Marjory Yates
—
Valerie Hillyard
Sheila Jellis

Sixth Row
Mary Stanford
Jean Sheppard
Ann Yates
Margaret Bryant
Jean Allen
Derek Buckingham
Ronnie Hall
—
—
—
—
—
Geoffrey Rowe
Harry Walters
Peter Janes
—
—
—
Robert Stone
Reg Smith
Peter Newton
Henry Biddlecombe
David Dunne
—
Gordon Hall
Ron Fuller
Peter Smith
Don Saunders
John Molyneaux
Michael Ward
Miss Mary Ireland
(Mrs Mountfort)

Fifth Row
Aubrey Cooper
Robert Oliver
Ivor Pett
Michael James
Stuart Stringer
Derek Tiller
Bryan Roberts
Ken Itzinger
Glynn Tilling
Harold Fletcher
— Yates
Peter Jellis
—
Dorothy Webb
Joyce Glynn

Maureen Ward
Anne Rowe
Edna Turney
Wendy Haynes
Betty Dunne
—
Margaret Little
Shirley Jeeves
Maragaret MacAlpine
Pamela Prince
Michael Bowers
Albert Peck
Brian Turney
Gordon Glynn
— Yates
Mrs Lang-Sadler

Fourth Row
Terry Fuller
Jim Wooliscroft
Roy Newton
—
Barry Buckingham
Cynthia Boutwood
—
Pat Parker
Ivy Bullen
—
Betty Jellis
Ann Fowler

Lorna Bowers?
—
June Hammond
—

—
Joy Brand
—
—
Pat Muckleston
Anne Nicholls
Pat Bland
Maureen Dyer
Paul Field
Brian Baker
Brian Davis
Philip Buckingham

Third Row
—
Peter Dunne
Tony Fuller
Janice Skeer
Madeline Ward
Billy Fowler
Donald Evans
—
Rosalie Hancox
Billy Pateman
Maurice Yates
Stanley Aston
Alan Richardson?
Leslie Payne
Kathleen Buckingham
—
Trevor Brown

Second Row
Thelma Oakley
Joan Willison
—
Mary Pateman
—
—
—
Michael Ward?
Margaret Willis
Austin Fleckney
Daphine Odell
—
—
Joyce Avery
Anne Tilling
—
—
—
George Day
Janet Pears
Jill Tiller
Micheal Gale
—
Janet Bowers
—
Jose Sheppard
Peter Fowler

Front Row
—
Pauline Buckingham
Alan Yates
Jean Stewart
Maureen Fuller
Peter Muckleston
Sylvia Saunders
Valerie Cleaver
—
Terry Smith
Raymond Buckingham
Jacqueline Jeeves
Yvonne Turney

Conger Hill, February 1940.

Every Shrove Tuesday, Toddington schoolchildren have raced up Conger Hill at 12 noon to listen to the old witch, who so legend has it, can be heard frying her pancakes in the kitchen under the hill. The earliest recorded mention is on 28 February 1865 when the headteacher recorded: 'Being Shrove Tuesday, according to ancient custom the children have a half holiday.' The tradition has now been revived again by St George's Lower School thanks largely to the Toddington Old Boys who revisited the hill in 2011. Pictured below are: Dave Stewart, Hedley Denmark, John Bryant, Tony Fuller, Julian Murch, Brian Compton, Len Smith. Representing the Old Scholars is Pauline Simmonds. They last scrambled up the hill in the 1940s and 1950s.

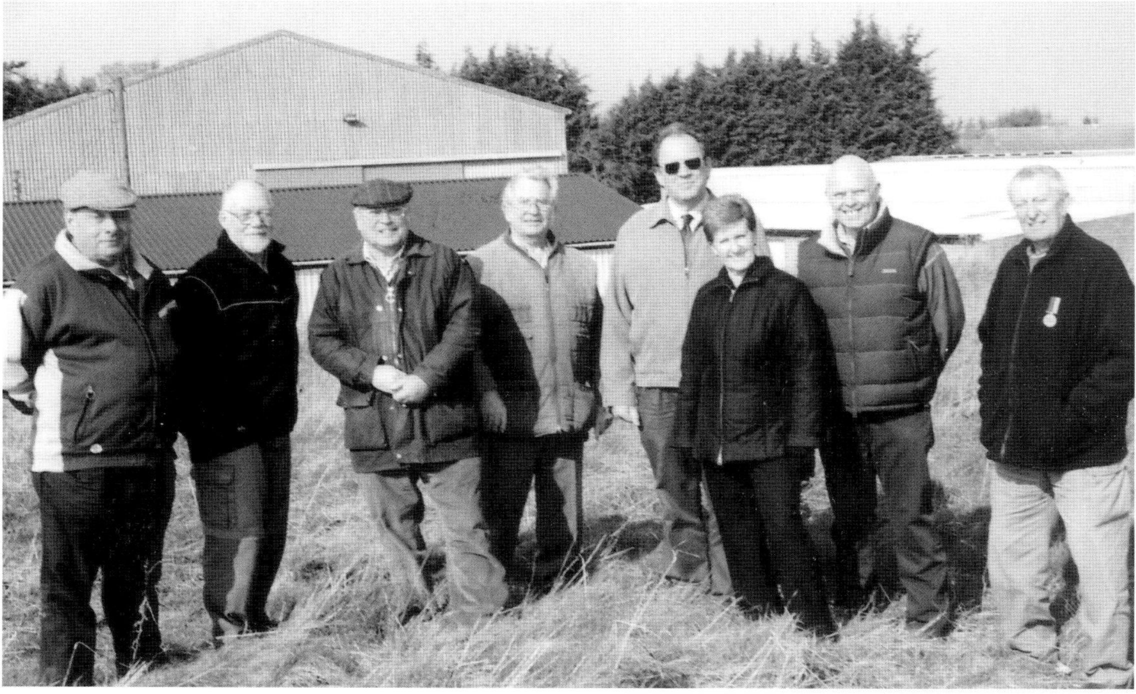

School Football Team, 1949-50.
Pictured include: Eric Caldecourt, Peter Winkworth, Stuart Stringer, Maurice Coles, Barry Buckingham, Bryan Roberts, Mick Gale.

This class shows teacher, Ruth Estelle Lang-Sadler née Alcock, who taught at the school in the 1930s,1940s and 1950s. She married in 1936 whilst still a teacher at the school. In the secondary schools if a woman got married she normally had to leave the school. The official reason for this was that married women's domestic obligations made them uncertain prospects for long term employment. The unofficial reason was that it allowed men to easily progress through the pay scales as the marriage bar meant a high turnover which prevented women accumulating pay increases.

Some of those pictured in this 1950s class are: Nicky Pett, Colin Bryson, James Biggs, Tony Courtney, June Blackmore, Gerald Payne, John Major and Angela Muckleston.

Standard II, 1951.
Back Row: T. Muckleston, E. Yates, J. Little, M. Whalley, -. , I. Single, - , J. Oliver, D. Buckingham.
Second Row: R. Blackmore, M. Bonner, J. Fowler, - , J. Oliver, R Kitchiner, S. Clifford, J.Parker ?, - , J. Whitbread.
Third Row: J. Manning, D. Muckleston , M.Hall, Mr K.O. Briggs, J. Pateman, R. Roberts, R. Patterson.
Front Row: A. Smith, D. Tew, P. Aston, J. Curtis, M. Brewer, P. Struggles.

Primary School caretaker, Amy Shepherd, pouring out tea at a school function to raise funds for a swimming pool.

Some of the staff used to do the crossword competitions during their break. They liked to solve the Daily Mail, Telegraph and occasionally The Times crossword. The main participants were Richard Dillingham, Amy Shepherd, Mary Mountfort and Andrée Morgan. Richard was good at literature, Mary was good at Biology and Andrée was good at French.

Amy was school caretaker for 26 years. Hazel Saunders was caretaker at the Secondary School .

Coke was the fuel used to heat the school. The author remembers helping Amy by filling a large scuttle and shovelling coke into the red hot interior of the stove. This was probably the next best thing to being the fireman on a train.

Sunday Schools

School competed with work for the child's time in Victorian times. One solution was to make use of the one day in the week the children's labour was not required, namely Sunday. For this reason children poured into Sunday schools, where they received training in basic literacy and numeracy as well as religious instruction.

The Primitive Methodists anniversary service was usually held about midsummer when the little chapel was packed to capacity. An improvised platform behind the rostrum held the Sunday School children. Now and then the service would be disturbed by a small child, overcome by the combined effects of a big Sunday lunch and the sweltering heat of the chapel, falling off the upper rows of the platform and landing, startled but usually uninjured on the rostrum.

The Baptists had James Horn who did much useful work in Chapel and Sunday School. He launched the Brotherhood movement in the village and for years presided over the Sunday afternoon meetings in the Town Hall. He preached the virtues of self-help and thrift.

The Wesleyans used to have their Sunday School anniversary on Easter Sunday. A special preacher was engaged and Wesleyans who had left the area came back for the annual reunion. The floor, galleries and even the aisles were crowded for the evening service. The side galleries were crammed with boys and girls from the Sunday School, clad in stiff or starchy suits or gowns. Special anthems and hymns and solo performances had been practised for weeks before the great day.

Mary Mountfort née Ireland recalls Sundays in the 1920s:

'I went to Sunday School at the National School. When you got older you went to the church for Confirmation Classes. Mum only used to go to Harvest Festival and not many more services because it was a long walk up and back. We used to have a flower festival in June. We used to take flowers and have a service in church and the flowers were taken to the sick people in Toddington. The door near the font was opened and we all used to walk in with the flowers and take them up to the altar. We used to learn a special hymn for the occasion and sometimes we did not do that good enough. Mr Wootton the headteacher and choirmaster used to take us for singing. We did not do plays like they do now. We just had the June festival. Nothing for Christmas - no nativity plays. Not many children used to go to Sunday School. Sunday School teachers included Claude Hawes and his brother Ken, Bertha Hyde and Dorothy Brazier. Mr and Mrs Wootton did not take Sunday School classes. We used to play up to the Sunday School teachers. We used to think that they were there to have their legs pulled.'

Beryl Hyde née Evans gives the following account of Sundays in the 1930s:

'Sunday was the day when we wore our best clothes, were generally on our best behaviour and went to Sunday School. On this day we never played boisterous games; the best we could do was a game with dolls and prams with my friend Joan. Sunday tea was a special treat with fruit from a tin and orange or lemon jelly, which always had to be eaten with bread and butter! This would be followed by a leisurely stroll to the cricket pitch down Park Road to watch a match being played.

There was a good attendance at all the different Sunday Schools and the anniversaries were something to be looked forward to. The Methodists always had theirs on Easter Sunday when the children paraded in their new outfits and special anthems were sung.

The Church Festival was held at the end of June. All the children, with their bunches of flowers, would line up on the path along the green and then proceed into church through the West Door, singing *All Things Bright and Beautiful*, to be met by the Rector, the Rev Hunt, a much respected gentleman.

The Primitive Methodists were noted for their hearty singing and the ranting of Mr "Sweepy" Clarke could be heard right up and down Leighton Road, particularly in the summer when they would leave the door wide open.

The Sunday School Treat was something looked forward to each year, and in fact was the only outing some of the poorer children had. Most Sunday Schools took their children to Wicksteed Park, Kettering and early in the morning the coaches would draw up along by the Town Hall. One by one we children arrived, with food and drink in one hand and a towel and bathing costume in the other. Wicksteed Park was an ideal place for our outing. All the slides and swings were free so the 6d we clutched tightly would buy two ice creams, a bar of chocolate and two goes on the water chute. By mid-day, tired of the swings and slides and with our money exhausted, it was time for a paddle in the pool and a rest in the warm sunshine.

At 3.30 we all congregated in the large rooms set aside especially for children on these occasions, with long rows of tables already laid out with egg and paste sandwiches and slices of fruit cake. The din was terrific and the tea was thoroughly enjoyed by all, although I'm not sure that today's youngsters would think very much of it.

By six o'clock, tired out and filthy dirty, we all clambered back into our coaches which were parked with dozens of others in the parking area and headed for home, arriving back in Toddington to be dragged home to bed.'

Priscilla Hart née Ireland gives the following account:

'I was allowed to cycle to Sunday School on Sunday afternoons. St George's Church had a large attendance of children in those days. The teachers I remember were Jack Smith, Mrs Nag Hobbs, Miss Gladys Lane, Miss Bertha Hyde, Miss Elsie Smith and Miss Dorothy Bates.

Dorothy taught the older children, and at the age of 16 we had instructions for confirmation with the Rev. Hunt at Denbigh House. A confirmed bachelor, the rector had accommodation at *Denbigh House*, the home of Mrs Barclay and he was allocated a rear room as his study. Sunday School treats came once a year when we travelled to Wicksteed Park near Kettering, on a double-decker bus, calling at Olney for fish and chips on our return. It was quite an occasion for children and adults, probably the longest distance some people travelled that year. Little Edwin who pumped the air for the church organ, used to sit in the front next to the driver - it was certainly a treat for him.'

Richard Dillingham recalls Edwin:

'I remember Edwin Babister, who was a dwarf. The Babisters were an old-established family in Toddington. He had a big head and body but very short legs. As a very young boy I remember him. I was told by somebody that they went on a Sunday School treat to the seaside and lost Edwin. They later found him on the beach surrounded by quite a crowd, passing the hat round!'

Sunday School teachers, about 1940. Standing: Connie Buckingham, Dorothy Brazier, Sarah Brewer, Sylvia Smith, Gladys Kingham, Olive Wilkins.
Sitting: Nancy Patterson, Bertha Hyde, Rev Hunt, Jack Smith (superintendent), Mrs Hobbs.

During the Second World War, Sunday School outings were organised by Dorothy Bates. Priscilla Hart née Ireland recalls going to Bedford for the annual Sunday School outing. The outing consisted of cycling to Harlington station and catching the train to Bedford for a visit to the embankment. Her parents were quite happy for Priscilla to go as they were under the watchful eye of Miss Bates. She only allowed them to hold hands as many of the school were of the age where they were discovering the opposite sex. The group were referred to as the 'Holding Hands Club'. Prior to the Second World War they had always been to Wicksteed Park in Kettering.

Sunday School, 1952. Pictured are: Sheila O'Dell, Richard Hancox, Jean Pateman, Roger Fox, Daphne Muckleston and Tom Shepherd. Classes were held in the National School by Bertha Hyde.

More people than nowadays attended church or chapel. A large number of children went regularly to Sunday School in the morning or afternoon. Sunday itself was a peaceful day with little traffic and only the newsagents shop open for a few hours in the morning.

Richard Dillingham MBE

These memories of Richard Dillingham MBE are based on an interview given in 1998 to the Toddington Historical Society. Mr Dillingham was headteacher of St George's School, Toddington for 27 years:

'In 1950 I was a peripatetic teacher. My base was at Stewartby, and I used to go to schools where they were short, particularly of heads. In 1950 I was sent to Roxton where I had a school of 60 five to eleven-year-old children on my own because the other teacher had fallen ill and there was no replacement. Large numbers were nothing new to me, because when I came out of college in 1935 I went to Stotfold Boys' School and had a class of 58 boys aged seven to nine, and of course strict discipline was the order of the day. When I went to Stewartby I had a class of 48 but that wasn't so bad because the classes were streamed. Anyway, to go back to Roxton there were no telephones and I received one afternoon a telegram asking me to call in at Shire Hall on the way home - which I did, and was interviewed by the Deputy Director, a man named Pinnock. He first of all said "Mr Dillingham, may I ask what is your religion?" I replied "C of E", and he said "Oh, we would like you to take over Toddington School. Are you willing to do that?" I said "Yes, of course, if you so require", and that was that. I had to turn up at Toddington the next day! As I was leaving I turned to him and said "You asked me my religion. Supposing I had not been Church of England, what then?" He replied "Oh, we would have wanted you to have taken over Clophill School". Well, the penny didn't drop then, but I later found out that Clophill was a Church of England School, and I could never understand why he said that I was to go to Toddington and not to Clophill. In effect, of course, it was much better to go to Toddington - but never mind!

Anyway, I turned up. Fred Young was head of the Secondary Modern School at the time; I was met by Mrs Fawcett, who made me very welcome and I settled in. Poor Bruce, whom I didn't know at all, had died during the summer. I suppose that he'd been ill and nothing had been done to prepare for the new term. We soon sorted things out and I went round to the staff. There were Miss Ashcroft, who became Mrs Joy, Kenneth Briggs, Mrs Saddler, Miss Troubridge, and a Miss Ryall. There were about 6 of us all told, and 192, if I remember rightly, on the roll.

I hadn't been there, I suppose a day, when a complaint came from the bus people. Children were brought from Tingrith by bus and the bus so-called conductress came to me and complained because one of the boys had been swearing on the bus. I called him to me and said "Barry, what's this I hear about you swearing on the bus?" and he replied "Not all the time, sir, not all the time!" So I had to let him off!

Things went on; Miss Ryall left - she was going to leave anyway, to get married - and then Mr Lamb was appointed. We were so crowded; there was no staff-room, no telephone, few washing facilities. The toilets were bucket lavatories in the middle of the playground - but in 1952 we did have new flush toilets. Fred Bonner, who was one of the managers, said "This is one of the best things that ever happened to Toddington", and he was probably right.

I have - and I must read it to you - something written on 23 November 1950, when I'd only been there a month or so: "Dear Sir, It has come to my knowledge today that the children in Mr Briggs' class are being taught to believe that the human races are descended from monkeys. I would have you know that I strongly disagree with this theory and strongly resent my boy John being taught the nonsense called anthropology. I would very much like to know if you approve of such teaching and also the Education Committee. Awaiting your reply." All Kenneth Briggs had said was "Of course, all you lot come from monkeys" and the boy had gone home and said this, and that was it.

Here's a nice little letter: "Last Wednesday, Gregory's "Tiny Tim" Club badge disappeared from his blazer and has not been found since. It was a new badge, and cost a shilling. Gregory is upset about this. On the same day he took to school a bag full of 24 marbles - some glass, some painted clay - altogether, a shilling's worth. I know that marbles is played by keeping what you win, but I assumed that he would only be playing against the tiny boys in his playground, against whom he would stand a fair chance. However, he told me that a big boy, named Kenneth Hall, came through into the end of the playground and said "Will you play marbles with me, Gregory? I'm not much good at it." So Gregory played against him and lost 23 out of 24 marbles. It seems rather mean for a big boy to have told Gregory that he wasn't much good at it, and anyway he shouldn't have been in the playground." Those are the sort of letters you get; they can be very funny.

We come to the Coronation, in 1953, which was a grand washout as far as things outside were concerned. I remember we had to erect a bandstand - that was the school stage, which we got down from the church from a room above the vestry; we lugged them all down, in the rain, and the whole thing was washed out. About four o'clock we repaired to *The Bell* where there was a roaring fire, and thawed ourselves out.

1954 was the Centenary and we had a week of various functions, starting with a church service. We had an Open Day for parents, a Sports Day, a Concert, and other events, with a Prize-Giving Day at the end. I produced a book with a foreword by Sir Frederick Mander, and I presume that he'd sent it up to *The Times* newspaper where it was reviewed, and on the strength of that I had letters requesting copies from all over the country. The main libraries wanted it, including the Bodleian and the Cambridge Library, the universities of Scotland, Wales and so on, and lots of interesting letters came in. I relied on the log books to provide information - for instance: "The stones in the playground do not seem much inclined to go in the ground. We borrowed a heavy roller today and in rolling the stones broke the crank"; that was in 1910. The admission registers and the log books should have started in 1854 but the first one we had was for 1863. It was recorded that my grandfather William Baker had received a prize for his writing. The first child was Mary Ann Barbey. Harry Russell told me this. I have on my sideboard a tankard won by my grandfather as a volunteer in the middle of the last century. It was a sort of Territorial Army; they used to go on parade and so forth. When the school was opened in 1854, that was the year that the Crimean War broke out and there was also a great freeze-up - there were icebergs on the Thames and they roasted oxen on the ice and things like that. They used to give "moral lessons". There's one here dated 1896: "Moral Lesson. Fathers in the hayfield". One wonders what form the lesson took, but could imagine it very well! I have various photographs; this one's a masterpiece. Punishment: "Three boys kept in for half an hour for blotting their copybooks". 14 November 1865: "Punished three of the elder boys this afternoon with a cane. Kept them in behind the rest for fox-hunting in school hours." One of the boys was punished in 1876 for kicking his teacher. 1918: "Punished WS and BG for indecent drawing and writing."; 18 November: "Punished JG for spitting in girls' faces". What a lark!

The children were dreadfully poor. Sometimes the fathers only earned two shillings a week - if they were employed - and they couldn't afford the two pence a week for school fees. They very often came to school without any breakfast at all; this is round about the 1860s. 5 November 1883: "I had to go up to the town to send the boys down to school". There's a lovely one here from 1885:

"TG excused school on account of want of sharpness". Things have changed now, of course, but even when I was head, dyslexia was hardly known. When I was at Stewartby there was a boy named Caves getting on for fourteen who couldn't write. One day one of his teachers said "I've done it: I've taught Caves to spell his own name", and I replied 'I don't believe it'. Caves was called; when asked to spell his name he said "C-v-e-a-s" - of course, the poor boy was dyslexic.

14 and 15 September 1899: "School dismissed at 2.55 pm as Doctor Grace (the famous cricketer), his son Lockwood and several other professional cricketers are playing a two-day match at The Park. On 22 July 1900 the boys had their cricket match in the grounds of Toddington Park on the splendid cricket pitch. Mr R.S. Sievier [the owner of Toddington Park] entertained the boys, the staff and all the onlookers to tea, and when the boys wished him "goodnight" he gave them 1s. [a shilling] each". That was money in those days! Also, the boys used to go off at all times following the hounds.

There were all kinds of red letter days. Here's one from 28 July 1911: "On Monday about 90 children were absent. They got up at 3am and went to various vantage spots to see if any of the aeroplanes taking part in the Great Race could be seen. Ten of the machines were visible; two came to grief, one at Streatley and one at Barton. A rush was made across the valley to Streatley". You can imagine it!

As early as the 1860s there was a half-holiday for Shrove Tuesday. There is no holiday these days, but the ancient custom was still carried out for many years. The tradition is that, if at noon you press your head to the ground at Conger Hill, you can hear the old woman frying her pancakes. The origin of this custom is obscure. We know the purpose of Conger Hill: it was a motte and bailey on which there was a small castle, probably of wood. There were bigger castles at Bedford and places like that, but they were built to keep the locals down. Then we come to Ascension Day, when the school used to go to church. The older children then were allowed to go up the tower, and the rest of the day was a holiday. Today I don't think the children are allowed to go to listen for the old woman; I asked why and was told it was in case of an accident since the school could be sued these days. That's probably right - some lawyer would get hold of it and sue. It's the same with Ascension Day, with taking the children across the road. One Shrove Tuesday, a lad went up Conger Hill with the rest of us but after school he went up on his own and he fell down and broke his leg; we wouldn't have been sued in those days. One year we were televised. It was a beautiful day.

Around 1954/5 there was an accident outside the school. Just up from the school there was a garage outside which they had put up a sign and a big thermometer and this boy, who was in the infant department, crossed the road to look at it then stepped back into the path of a lorry and was killed. I can remember it; it was an awful day. I had to go there and virtually stand over the body, in the road, and direct traffic past it until an ambulance arrived and things like that. The boy's mother was expecting a child and it was a hot day, and instead of coming right down to the school to collect the child she had stayed at a seat on the Green, and of course this happened. On the strength of that, it was realised that traffic was becoming more and more hazardous. It was decided that it would be better if children did not come down the main road but went round the back along a path which leads along the edge of the cemetery, past the old school, to Conger Hill, and out into Conger Lane by Buckinghams' farm. The fact was that the children might be afraid of Buckingham's cows; so instead of a lollipop lady or warden, a cow warden was appointed. His job was to see that the children got past the cows safely, and keep the path clean from the cows! The man who was appointed was named Hucklesby, nicknamed "Diggles". He appeared on *What's My Line?*, and the panellists didn't get him.

I can remember when the Reverend Fell was the Rector and there was all this business about the state of the old building down Station Road. One night, the lintel over one of the windows fell down. Had it fallen during the day, it could have hurt a child. We got people out from Shire, now County Hall, and complained, but nothing was done. This was because it was a church school and not a council school, and so it took a back seat. All kinds of legal paraphernalia had to be gone through.

We had the centenary, and the school got bigger and bigger. As numbers grew we were always pressed for room. Classes were large, but since our methods were largely traditional, the desks were in rows and class teaching prevailed - there is now a swing back to this. For many years children took the 11+ exam which largely tested the children's basic knowledge of the three Rs. Parents were given written reports which were based on standardised tests on the three Rs. We were very successful; often as many as 20% were offered places at Grammar or High Schools. Sport was always a priority, for children love it. Here too we were very successful, winning the Bedfordshire Primary Cup at football, and with many successes in Athletics. In the later years, we also held an inter-schools swimming gala.

When I first arrived the school roll was 192; by 1955 it was 250; by the time I left, in 1977, it was 550. In 1963 Parkfields School opened and as we were bursting at the seams, part of the school took over the old secondary modern school building in Leighton Road. We left the infants down at the old school and took the sevens to elevens up to Leighton Road; we used the old Primitive Chapel as a hall. There we were until 1967 when our new school (now St George's Lower School) opened in Manor Road. There were ten classrooms, two of them quite small - they were called "practical rooms" - but there were 440 on roll, so it doesn't need a mathematical genius to work out that this was going to mean classes of 44. So what did we do? We sent part of the school back to Leighton Road. We also had no end of temporary classrooms. We had a swimming pool, which is now filled in, which is a shame, but there was insufficient money to keep it going.

We once held a parent-teacher function in the Club with the usual raffle. I asked the Secretary to make the draw - she drew her own ticket. I shook it all up, held it aloft and she drew mine. "Wangle" they all shouted, so I asked anyone to come up and make the next draw. A young woman came up and promptly drew her own ticket. Extraordinary! (No such luck with the Lottery.)

In the early days of the PTA an outing to Windsor was arranged on mid-summer's day ending with a river trip from Windsor to Marlow. As soon as we got aboard there was a terrific thunderstorm and during the trip 2 inches of rain fell.

The school managers in 1954 were:

Rev S. Fell (Chairman)

Mrs L.B.M. Fawcett	Mrs E.K. Hart	Mr S.J. Little
Mr G.H. Coles	Mr H. Russell	Mr D. Hyde

They were a good lot; I don't think we ever fell out - we just discussed things rationally.'

School governors or managers, 1954: Denis Hyde, Harry Russell, Mrs Fawcett, Ella Hart, George Coles. Not pictured are the Rev Fell, and S.J. Little. They had the task of seeing that the school was 'conducted in a proper manner'. They were spared the financial worries affecting the school unlike the managers prior to 1947 who 'had a most trying time in raising money to keep the building, playground etc in repair'.

Class, about 1952. Back row: Raymond Buckingham, Raymond Smith, John Baker, John Pett, David Caldecourt, Malcolm Chapman, Peter Bryson, David Wooliscroft, David Croucutt.
Third row: Sheila Russell, Betty Curtis, Iris George, Rosemary Willis, Kay Parker, Susan Marlow, Margaret Smith, Bernice Chapman, Pat Carr, Joy Boutwood.
Second row: Kenny Hall, Pauline McAlpine, Syhlvia Lawsey, Mrs Joy, Janet Buckingham, Gill Major, George Stewart.
Front row: Paul Harris, Alan Russell, Terry Bowers, Brian Tiller, Richard Bryant, Paul Bloomer, Barry Lee, David William.

One of the subjects Mrs Joy taught to the class was knitting.

CLASS I. (10-11)

	9.10	9.25	9.50	10.45	11.0	11.35	12.10	1.30	2.5	2.35	2.45	3.15 3.45
Monday	Assembly and Regis. **9.30**	R.I. **10.0**	Hist-ory Arith B.B.C.		Composition			Drama	Literature		Girls : Needlework Boys : Games	
Tuesday	Spelling	Religious Service (B.B.C.)	Arithmetic		Geography	P.T.		History	English (Study Reading)		Boys : Handwork Girls : Country Dancing	
Wednesday	Assembly and Regis.	R.I.	Arithmetic		Geography	Reading Inter-pretation		Hand-writing	Music		Boys : Practical Maths. Girls : Needlework	
Thursday	Assembly and Regis.	R.I.	English Compo-sition		History	P.T.		Art			Boys : Gardening Girls : Games	
Friday	Spelling	R.I.	Arithmetic		Mechanical Reading	P.T.		Nature Study			Choir and Literature	**3.30** Assembly

RECEPTION CLASS. (5-6)

	9.10	9.25	9.50	10.10	10.45	11.0	11.35	12.10	1.30	2.5	2.35	2.45	3.10 3.30
Monday	Regis. and Assembly	Dinner Money & Bank	P.T.	Number		English			Activities			Nature	
Tuesday	Regis. and Assembly	R.I.	P.T.	Number		English			Activities			Music	Story
Wednesday	Regis. and Assembly	R.I.	P.T.	Number		English			Activities			Story	Music
Thursday	Regis. and Assembly	R.I.	B.B.C. Music & Movement	Number		English			Activities			Music	Story
Friday	Regis. and Assembly	Hymn Singing	**10.25** Number			Music	English		Activities			Dramatic Work	

Timetable, 1954

Below: Mr R. Dillingham (head), Mrs.R. E. Lang-Sadler, Mrs D.M.Wootton, Mr A. F. Brook

Teachers sitting above, 1954: Mr F.R. Lamb, Miss E.O.W. Troubridge, Mrs W. Joy.

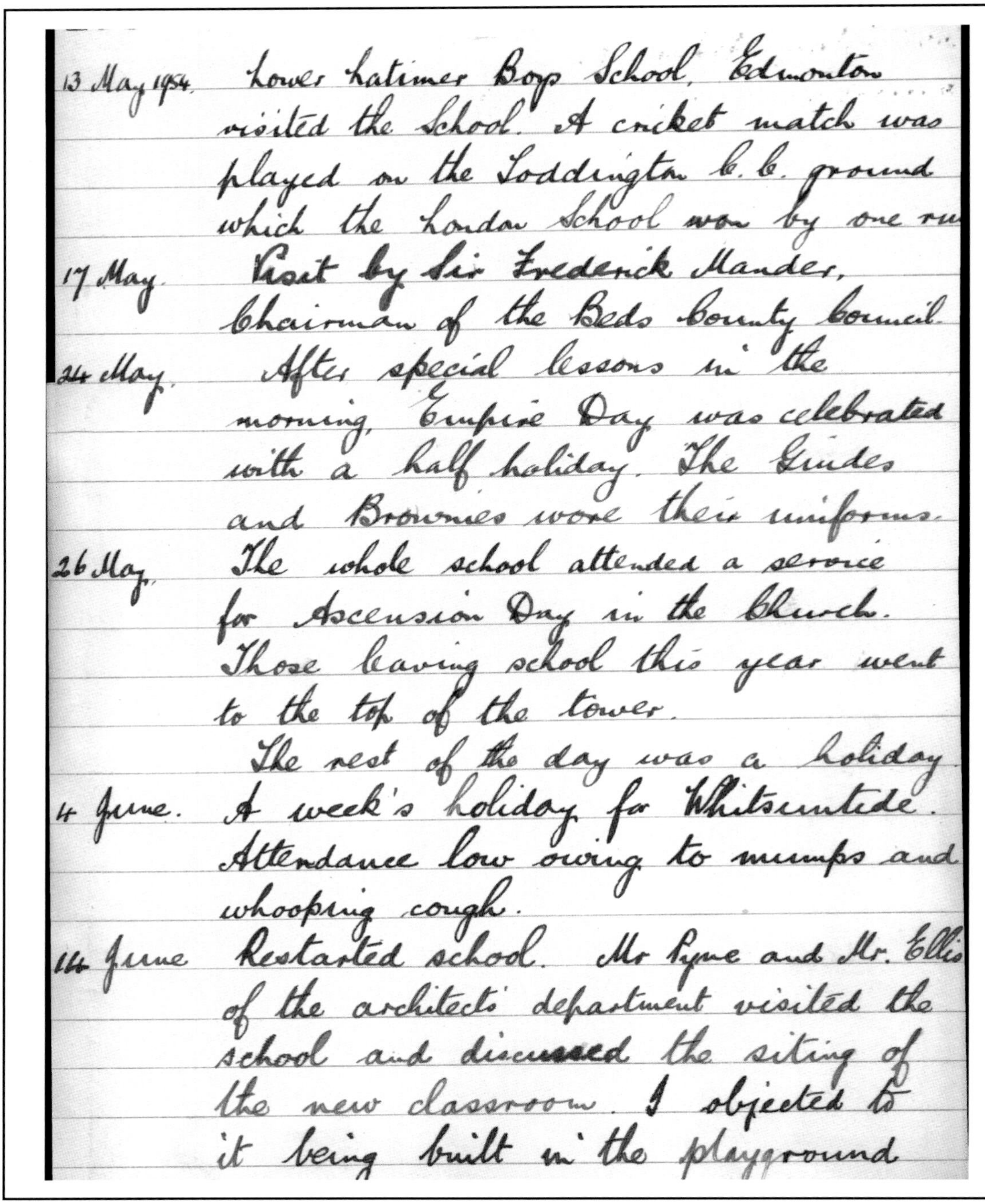

13 May 1954. Lower Latimer Boys School, Edmonton visited the School. A cricket match was played on the Toddington C.C. ground which the London School won by one ru

17 May. Visit by Sir Frederick Mander, Chairman of the Beds County Council.

24 May. After special lessons in the morning, Empire Day was celebrated with a half holiday. The Guides and Brownies wore their uniforms.

26 May. The whole school attended a service for Ascension Day in the Church. Those leaving school this year went to the top of the tower.

The rest of the day was a holiday.

4 June. A week's holiday for Whitsuntide. Attendance low owing to mumps and whooping cough.

14 June Restarted school. Mr Pyne and Mr. Ellis of the architects' department visited the school and discussed the siting of the new classroom. I objected to it being built in the playground

School log books were the record of daily activities in the school kept by the headteacher. Records had to be kept from 1862. Here is a page from Mr Dillingham's school log book for events that happened in May and June 1954.

Note Empire Day used to be celebrated on 24 May every year. On this day in the 1930s the children used to march round the playground saluting the Union Flag. In this 1954 log it was recorded that special lessons were given in the morning with the afternoon being a holiday. The Guides and Brownies wore their uniform to school. On Ascension Day a church service was held for the whole school with the school leavers being allowed to ascend to the top of the church tower. The rest of the day was a holiday.

Prize Giving, 1954. Sir Frederick Mander presents a prize to John Baker. Mr E. Page, Mr D. Hyde (school manager), Rev S. Fell (chairman of managers) and Mr R. Dillingham (head) are also present.

Boys sitting on bank at right include: G. Chalmers, J. Manning, I. Single, M. Lowe, D. Kempton, K. Hall. The girls sitting in front of the boys include: J. Oliver, R. Kitchiner, G. Major.

Left: Sir Frederick Mander, Chairman of the County Council, presents a prize to Geoffrey Holman who is wearing shorts and long socks. It was not until boys went to a secondary school that they wore long trousers.

Subject Analysis	Age / *Classes*	10-11 I	9-10 II	8-9 III	7-8 IV	6-7 V	5-6 VI
Speech Training, Recitation and Drama		30	30	65	60	...	...
Listening to Good English	... ...	30	45	55	65	...	...
Reading: Mechanical	... ...	35	75	95	145	...	...
Interpretation	... ...	35	30	30	...	...	...
Study	... ...	30	30	...	...	...	...
Composition, Oral and Written		125	115	155	95	...	...
Spelling	... ...	30	30	55	85	...	...
TOTAL ENGLISH		315	310b 355g	485	450	440	425
Handwriting	... ...	30	70	65	95	40	...
History	... ...	90	65	60	25	...	...
Geography	... ...	70	70	60	30	...	...
Nature Study and Science...	... ...	60	75	60	60	75	45
Arithmetic	... ...	185 60b	195 45b	240	235	150	175
Art	... ...	60	60	60	60	60	...
Handwork (Boys only)	... ...	60	60	70	60	110	...
Needlework (Girls only)...	... ...	120	120	70	60	...	...
Gardening (Boys only)	... ...	60	60	...	...	...	...
Music	... ...	75	60	55	65	110	130
Physical Education	... ...	165 60g	160	110	120	120	100
Religious Instruction	... ...	130	130	130	165	80	75
Registration and Assembly	... ...	85	85	85	85	100	100
Optinional or free activities. (Includes Art, handwork, writing, sensory appartus, etc.) ...	... ...	...	...	...	...	70	300
Collection of money, etc. ...	... ...	...	...	...	...	20	25
TOTAL TIME IN MIN.		1,450	1,450	1,450	1,450	1,375	1,375

These tables show how the school week was spent by the children starting at five years and ending their last year at eleven. They were a guide for the teacher who had a definite syllabus to try and cover during the school year as some lessons would require more or less time.

School Centenary Concert, 1954. Pictured are: Denis Hyde, Alec Kingham, Ivor Pett, Trevor Brown and Harry Mourne.

The School Netball team, 1955-6. This team did not lose a match. Pictured D. Withington, Miss E.O.W. Troubridge, S. Randall on the back row. Front row: S. Nichols, A. Muckleston, M. Davis (captain), V. Horning, J. Blackmore.

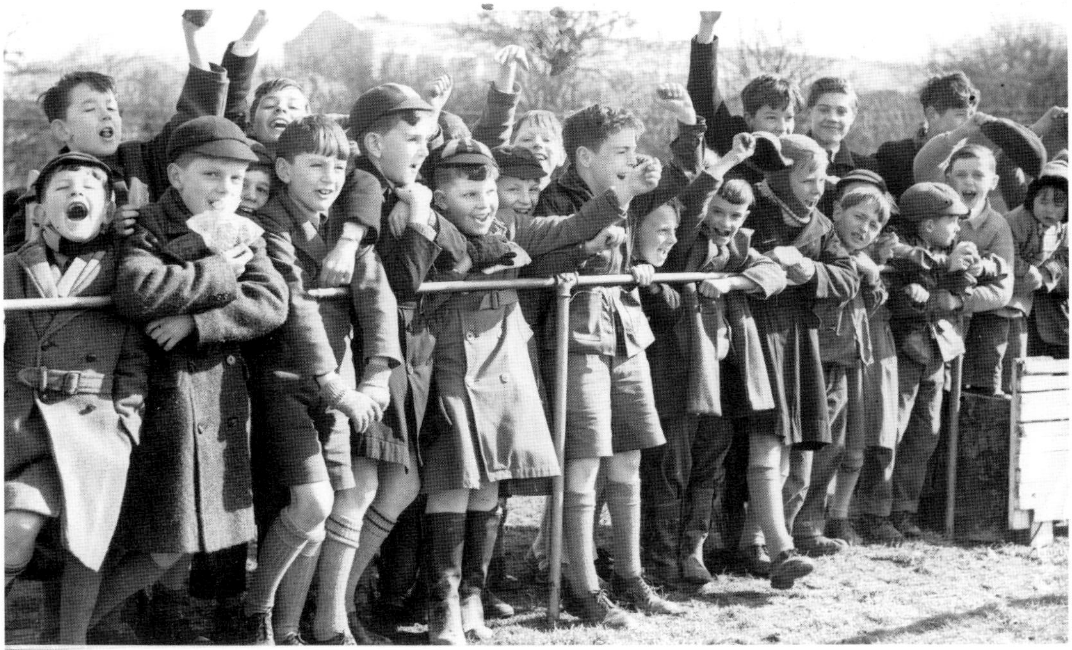

Spectators shouting for their school at the 'Cup' Final on Dunstable Town Ground, 10 March 1956. The school football team drew 0-0 in the final against Dunstable Ashton School. Each school held the cup for 6 months. The school team was: F. Holman (goal), T. Shepherd (right back), J Peck (left back), G. Chalmers (left half), N Buckman (centre half), P. Fletcher (right half), C. Single (outside right), C. Maughan (inside right-captain), T. Yates (centre forward), I. Russell (inside left) and M. Edwards (outside left).

Below: The team 1955-56 with the winning cup. Back Row: Richard Dillingham (head-teacher) Norman Buckman, George Chalmers, Tom Shepherd, Frank Holman, Donald Nelson, Jimmy Peck, Chris Single, Alan Brooker (games [PE] teacher).

Front row: Peter Fletcher, Martin Edwards, Colin Maughan, Tony Yates, Ian Russell.

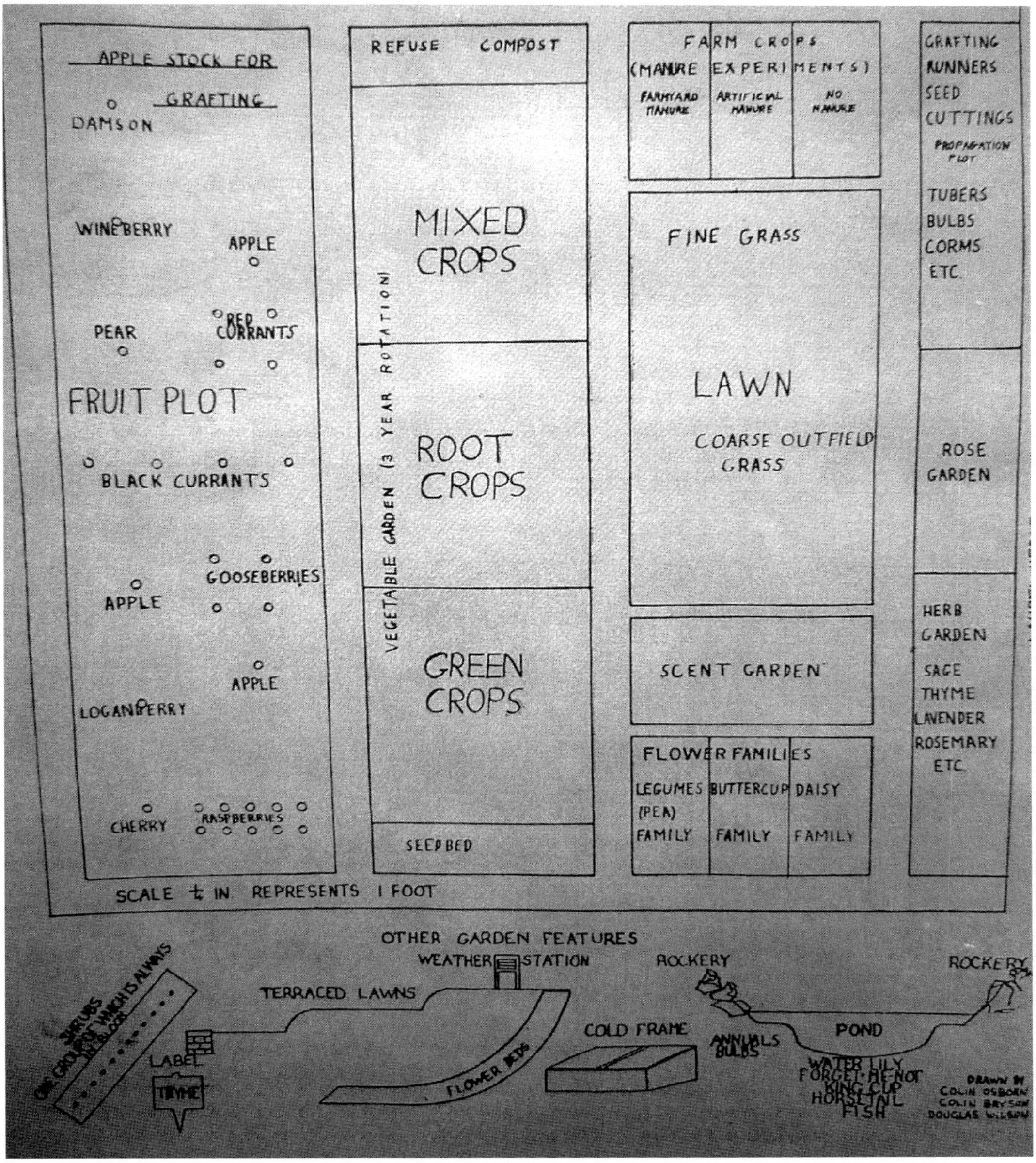

In April 1956, the school garden was again featured in the BBC broadcast to Country Schools. The plan above was drawn by three pupils, Colin Osborn, Colin Bryson and Douglas Wilson and included in the BBC pamphlet. In a previous broadcast in May 1954 the gardens were described in some detail lasting a quarter of an hour. A visitor commented in turn on the vegetable plot, the fruit plot, the lawn, the farm crops, the flower family plot, the propagation plot, the rose garden, the herb garden and the flower borders.

1956 Class, teacher Miss Troubridge. In April 1955 the dinner numbers had to be limited to 130 (half the school, as 260 on the roll). This necessitated sending children home to dinner whose mothers were not at work and who lived nearest the school.

To begin with dinners were served at the Council School and pupils were walked crocodile style up to the school in Leighton Road. It was only later that dinners were served in the school classrooms at Station Road.

J. Sheppard and G. Holman winning the wheelbarrow race for 7-8 year olds, Sports Day 1956.

Prize Giving Day, 25 July 1957. This took place on the terraces outside the new classrooms. The headteacher reported that the number on the roll had increased from 253 to 300 during the year. He also reported that employers were becoming more selective and as time went on applicants with the necessary qualifications would get the better jobs. Mr Neale, chairman of the Toddington Old Boys, gave a humorous speech. 'Make your school life a happy adventure' was his advice to children. 'A happy school was a successful school.'

The audience are seen here in the playground on this very hot July afternoon. Teachers: Miss S. Little (back), Mrs D.M. Wootton (centre), Mrs P Broome (front). Selections were given by the school choir. The Briden Sports Cup, The Relay Cup, The Football Shield and the S.J. Little Netball Cup were all presented to the winning teams. The closing hymn, which was also the school hymn, was Jesus, Good above all Others *followed by* God save the Queen. *The school hymn contained the line 'Give us Grace to Persevere'. 'Persevere' was the school motto which formed part of the design on the blazer badge. Refreshments were provided by the Home School Association and parents were invited to visit the classrooms to see the children's work.*

Reg Neale, chairman of the Toddington Old Boys' Association, presents Jennifer Parrott and Colin Nash with the William Hyde Awards, 1958. Jennifer and Colin were given a book each as reward for being nominated as the girl and boy most likely to make the best citizen. They were able to chose the book they wanted prior to prize giving.

Mrs Broome's class, 6 July 1957. These 40 pupils learnt to read by using Janet and John *books which used repetition of words to learn eg See John run, see Janet run. Although the books were quintessentially English, the author Rona Munro was from New Zealand and the books were first published in the USA. Instead of phonics, they relied upon the new method of 'Look and Say', where children learned whole words at once. Each simple sentence was accompanied by a bright, colour picture of the two children playing out of doors.*

Leavers Summer 1957 and 1958

P. Brown, M. Major to Luton Grammar School ;

R. Rowles, G. Manning - Dunstable Secondary Technical School

C. Dillingham - Bedford High School

L. Galloway, J. Parrott, W. Smith - Luton High School

C. Nash, R. Ball, P. Brewer, L. Brown, R. Burman, T. Chapman, M. Edwards, R. Fox, R. Galloway, A. Hucklesbury, M. Jeffries, B. Jones, D. Lewsey, R. Robinson, J Rogers, I .Russell, M. Shepherd, M. McLellan, S.Bainton, A. Buckingham, G. Fowler, M. Harris, L. Heeps, R .Hucklesby, S. Itzinger, S. Millard, S. Patterson, C. Stewart, S. Day to Toddington County Secondary Modern School.

The following year the percentage passing the 11-plus increased from 21% to 43%. The boys now went to Dunstable Grammar School: Christopher Atkinson, Paul Hobbs, Brian Kitchiner, Julian Murch, Roger Nicholls, Patrick Sheehan, Ian Warburton, Paul Wiley and John Wren.

Luton High School: Christine Burch, Mary Childs, Susan Fellowes, Shirley Fowler, Carole Pateman and Mary Coles.

Kingsbury School, Dunstable: Arthur Johnson, David Richardson, Paul Rowe, Reginald Stanley, David Yeomans.

Winners of the Dunstable and South Beds Schools Junior Cup Competition, 1958. The team won every match during the season. Back row: R. Dillingham (headteacher), A. Simmonds, K. Smith, P. Ward, C. Armstrong, C. Atkinson. Front row: P. Sheehan, J. Yates, P. Hobbs, A. Johnson (captain), R Nicholls, C. Marlow, W. Stanley.

The Dunstable Gazette *gave the following account:*

'The score was 0-0 at half time. During the second half Stanley broke straight through the defence and hit the ball into the corner of the net. With four minutes left Smith the inside-left, made it 2-0 with a hard drive. From the kick off the opponents Highfields scored. The final whistle went soon after, the score being 2-1 to Toddington. The mayor of Dunstable Ald W.T. Lack presented the cup to the Toddington captain.'

School Numbers

'There is no record of attendance at the opening of the School. We must remember that it was not until 1870 that children between the ages of 5 and 10 were "compelled" to go to school.

Also children were admitted at three and in general it seems that parents were anxious for their children to start early, but were not so particular when they became older and able to do work.

A few figures will show the growth of the school:

1873	120	1914	190
1876	150	1919	191
1878	204	1926	173
1881	235	1928	201
1882	250	1936	214
1884	265	1943	195
1890	301	1945	235
1895	280	1947	204
1903	305	1951	222
1906	262	1954	250
1911	228		

National School 1854-1954, by Richard Dillingham.

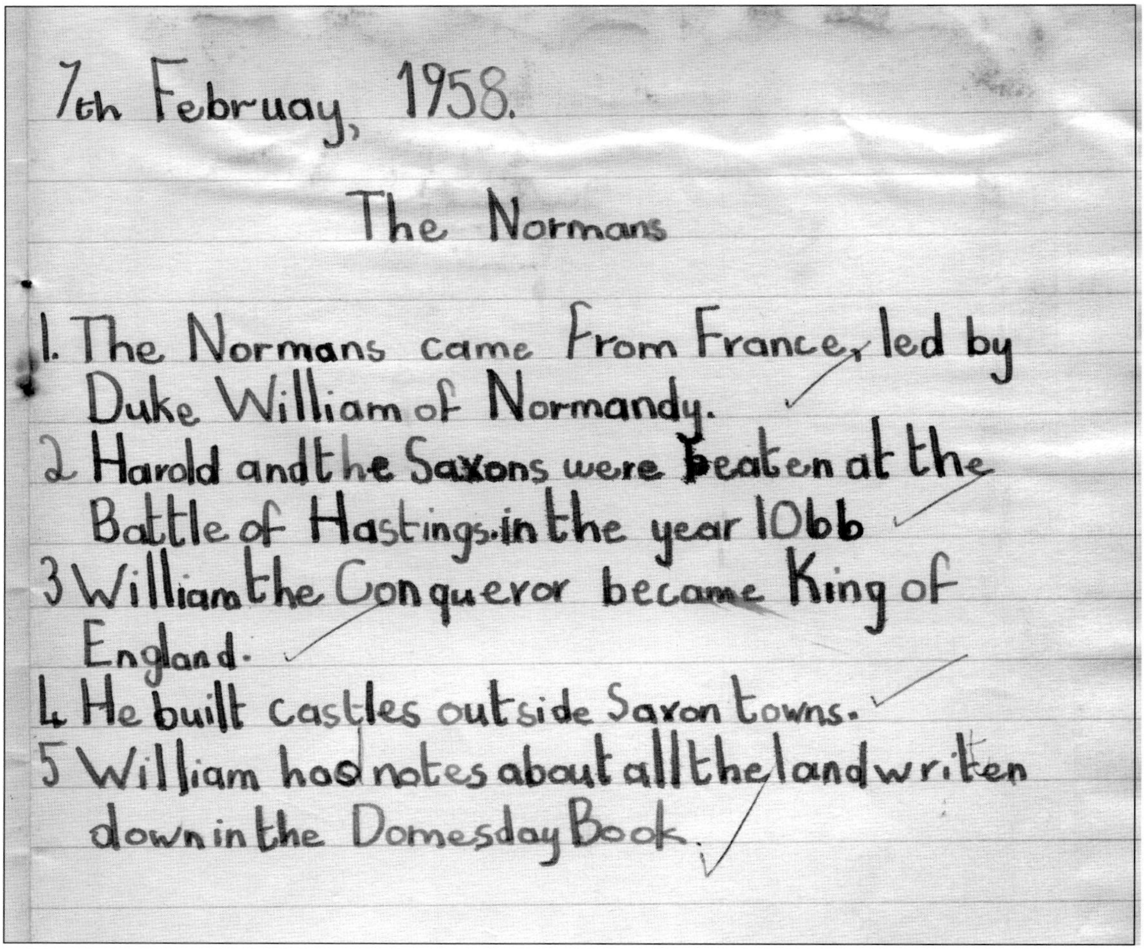

7th Februay, 1958.

The Normans

1. The Normans came from France, led by Duke William of Normandy.
2 Harold and the Saxons were beaten at the Battle of Hastings in the year 1066
3 William the Conqueror became King of England.
4 He built castles outside Saxon towns.
5 William had notes about all the land written down in the Domesday Book.

History notes written with ink in an exercise book, 7 February 1958, by a seven-year-old. Pupils were expected to write with a pencil before progressing to a dip pen. One had to dip the pen in the inkwell after every word or two, and if you were not careful you could end up making a frightful mess. The problem was that the ink took quite a while to dry, and unless you were incredibly careful you would end up with a lot of splodges and smears. Excess ink was removed from the nib by using the inside edge of the inkwell. Blotting paper was used when necessary; for instance if you wanted to turn the page to carry on writing. There was a knack to writing with ink. Make your strokes the wrong way and the nib would twist and spray minute droplets of ink on the page.

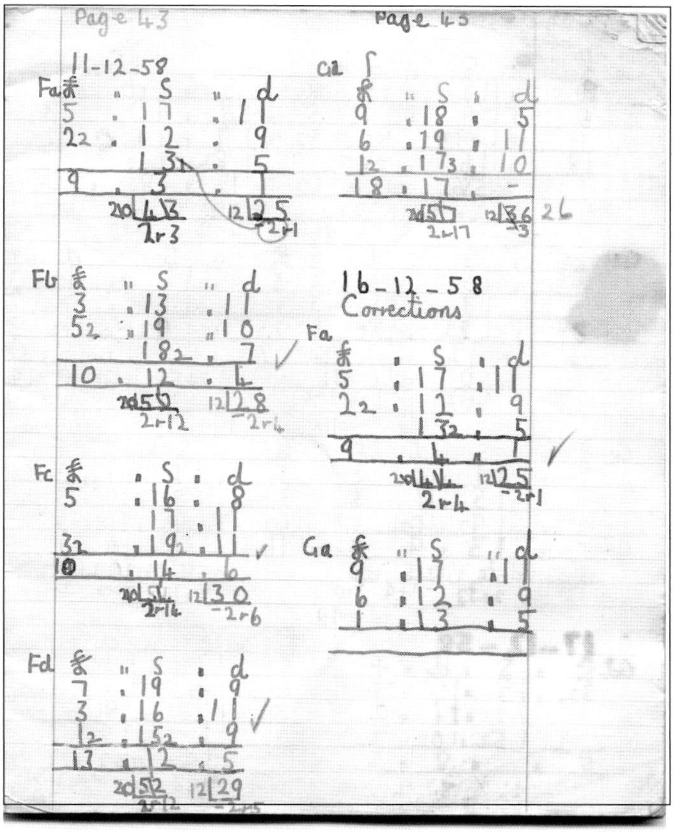

An eight-year-olds maths book dated 11 December 1958. In a recent reversal the modern methods of teaching maths, such as the grid method, have been abandoned in favour of the tried and tested system of adding up, subtracting, multiplying and dividing in vertical rows as seen in these pictures.

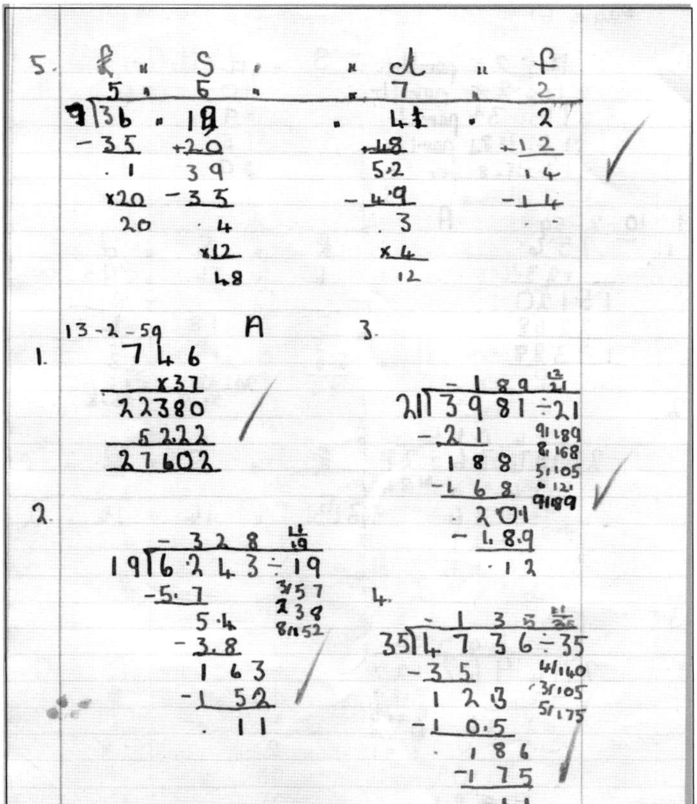

Bedfordshire's Competitive Music Festival, March 1959. During the week participants who sang or danced as well as choirs and orchestras were all assessed by adjudicators who were specialists in their particular fields. Entries came from places as far apart as Letchworth and Nottingham.

Toddington Voluntary Primary School Prize Giving Day, Thursday 9 July 1959 at 2.30pm.

Chairman: Mr R.D. Cawley
Prizes presented by Mr B.J. Hyde JP (chairman Luton Rural District Council)
Introductory remarks: Mr R.D. Cawley
Choir selected from: Solitude, My Bonny Cuckoo, The Green Rushes, Marianina and Berry Picking.
Report by the Headteacher: Mr R. Dillingham.
Presentation of Prizes:

Class 1A	Eileen Simmonds, Jacqueline Kitchener, Geoffrey Harbottle, Albert Errington.
Class 2	Rodney Smith, Rita Kennard, Margaret Conquest, Shirley Smith, Alan Turney.
Class 3	John Bryant, Melvin Silver, Margaret Pay, Linda Horning.
Class 1V a	Brian Cawley, Garry Banks, Stephanie Webster, David Jamieson.
Class1Vb	Charlotte Ellis, Corinne Pateman, Nicholas Turney, Michael Walters.

The William Hyde Awards presented by the Toddingon Old Boys:
Heather Pears, Christopher Day.

The Bruce M. Wootton Memorial Scripture Prizes:

Class 1	Vivien Smith.
Class 2	Adrian Purser.
Class 3	Mary Mountfort.
Class 4a	Barbara Boutwood, Ian Simmonds.
Class 4b	Robert Cooper, Richard Peachey.

Music Trophy awarded by Mrs R. Wegener: Christine Waters.
The Dr R.F. Fawcett Memorial History Prize: Margaret Dillingham, David Ward.
Attendance Prizes: awarded by Mr S.J. Little:
Christopher Armstrong, Geoffrey Holman, Roger Major, John Sheppard, Lesley Aldred, Lynda Turney, Janet White, Lyn Anderson, Kathleen Bainton, Kathleen Fowler, Ann Neal, Mary Mountfort, Philip Fowler, Ian Alan Stewart.
School Prizes awarded by Brooke Bond's Tea:

Handwriting:	First: Margaret Anderson.
	Second: Andrew Single.
Art:	First: Margaret Dillingham.
	Second: Barrie Rowles.
Infants Art	First: Robin Brewer.
	Second: Raymond Baker.

Art Prize awarded by Mr E. Warburton: Stanley Clark.
Art Awards; Stanley Clark, Margaret Anderson, Margaret Dillingham.
Prizes to Scholarship Winners awarded by Mr R.S. Allen and Mr G. Coles:
Christopher Armstrong, Eric Brown, Richard Burrows, Stanley Clark, Christopher Day, Kenneth Janes, Roger Major, John Sheppard, Peter Deary, Margaret Anderson, Sheila Atkinson, Margaret Dillingham, Kathleen Lewzey, Heather Pears, Vivien Smith, Carole Stapleton.
English Prizes awarded by the Home School Association:
Heather Pears, Angela Palmer, John Bryant.
Swimming Certificates:
15 yds Jennifer Cook, Andrew Tilling, Robert Millard, Heather Pears, Sheila Atkinson.
Nature Prize: Lesley Hyde.
Geography Prize: Susan Hoar.
Progress Prize: John Stanley.

Class 2 with Mrs Joy, June 1960. Back Row: Robert Edmonds , Stephen Martin, David Smith, Michael Bird, Mark Bray, Aubrey Russell, Norman Bates, Michael Smith , David Jamieson.
Third row: Jacqueline Sendall, Jennifer Lamb, Valerie Lewsey, Susan Walters, Eileen Guttridge, Patricia Battams, Cathrine Ward, Mary Stanley, Helen Boffey, Mary Brazier, Vivien Green.
Second Row: Barbara Boutwood, Stephanie Webster , - , Lorna Brand, Pauline Yates, Isabel McLellan, Nicola Wiggett, Carol Brand, Joanna Harris, Kathleen Holman, Linda Janes (standing):
Front row: Hedley Denmark, Patrick McLaughlin, David Newitt , Peter Bainton , Richard Hart, Stephen Petryszyn, Ian Simmonds, Brian Cawley.

Pupils who took part in the Bedfordshire Competition Music Festival.

Mr Lamb's Class, June 1960.
Back row: Graham Hansford, Stephen Bleaney , Stephen Blackman, Albert Errington, Peter Smith, David Pay, Robin Katz , Barry Williams and Clive Green.
Third row: Susan Hoar, Jill Wiley, Angela Palmer, Shirley Smith, Margaret Conquest, -, Lesley Hyde, Jennifer Marlow, Jane Evans, Catriona Cameron, Linda Coles, Patricia Barnes.
Second row: Ruth Weatherly, Cecilia Pay, Mary King, Eileen Simmonds, Linda Turney, Linda Friend , Christine Smith, Patricia Timms, Elizabeth Smith, Judith Bates, Ann Neal.
Front row: James Boffey, Stephen Bromwich, John Bryant, John Stanley, Geoffrey Harbottle, Geoffrey Holman, Alex McLellan, David Warby, Margaret Pay and Linda Horning.

2011 Reunion of the 9-10 year old ('Nappy Wearers') . Pictured are: Front row (left to right) Hedley Denmark, Paul Bryant and John Bryant. Back row: Yvonne Keeble, Val Lewsey, Sandra Clark, Pauline Yates, Ruth Weatherley, Lesley Squires, Linda Horning, Linda Coles, Catriona Cameron and Vivienne Morgan.

Netball Team, 1960. Back row: Lesley Hyde, teacher Mrs Joy, Margaret Pay. Front row: Patricia Timms, Barbara Kent, Eileen Simmons, Judith Bates and Cecelia Pay.

Teacher Mrs Joy with her class, about 1959. By then most of the classes had 40 or more children and 230 stayed to dinners in the classrooms.

The teaching staff encouraged generations of schoolchildren to develop to their full potential. This was accomplished with very little resources.

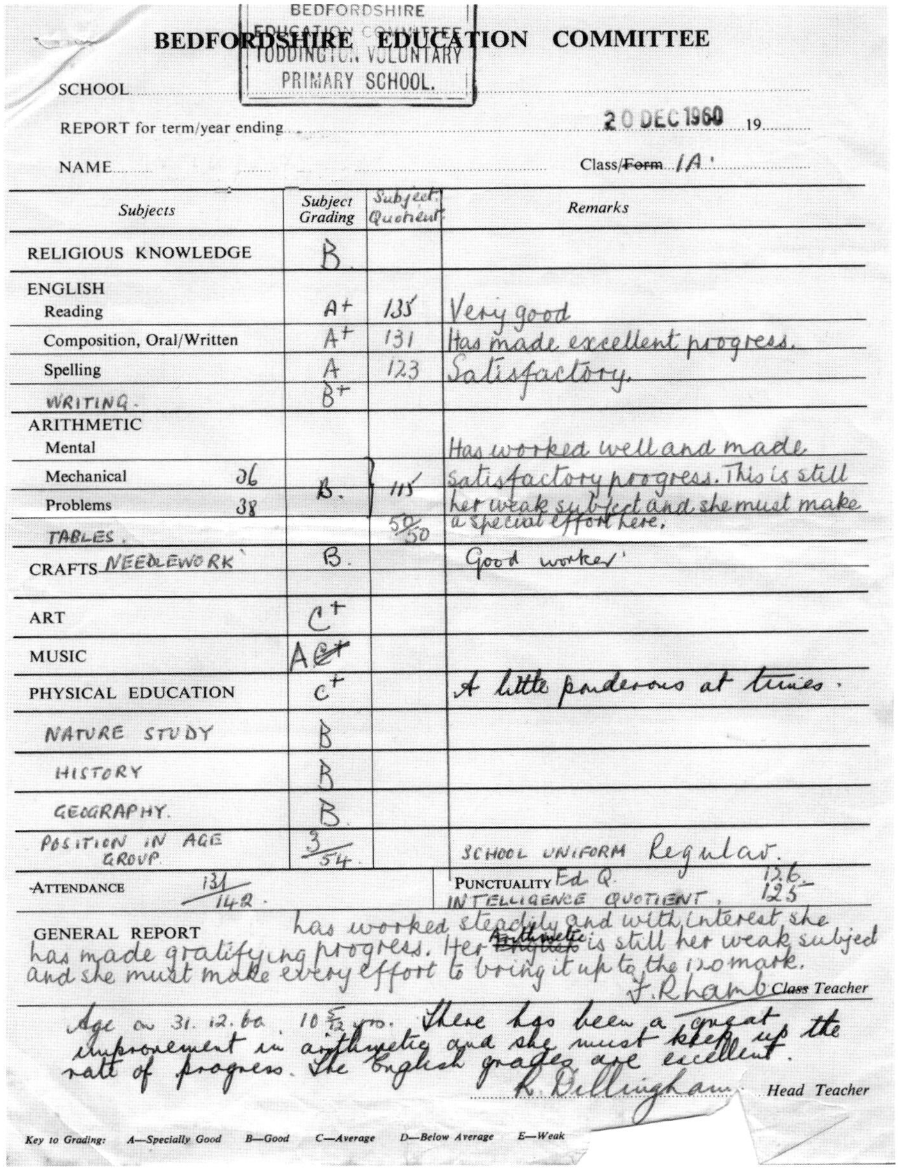

BEDFORDSHIRE EDUCATION COMMITTEE

SCHOOL [stamp: BEDFORDSHIRE EDUCATION COMMITTEE TODDINGTON VOLUNTARY PRIMARY SCHOOL.]

REPORT for term/year ending 20 DEC 1960 19

NAME Class/~~Form~~ 1A'

Subjects	Subject Grading	Subject Quotient	Remarks
RELIGIOUS KNOWLEDGE	B.		
ENGLISH			
Reading	A+	135	Very good
Composition, Oral/Written	A+	131	Has made excellent progress.
Spelling	A	123	Satisfactory.
WRITING.	B+		
ARITHMETIC			
Mental			Has worked well and made
Mechanical 36	B.	115	satisfactory progress. This is still
Problems 38			her weak subject and she must make
TABLES.		50/50	a special effort here.
CRAFTS NEEDLEWORK'	B.		Good worker'
ART	C+		
MUSIC	A ~~C+~~		
PHYSICAL EDUCATION	C+		A little ponderous at times.
NATURE STUDY	B		
HISTORY	B		
GEOGRAPHY.	B.		
POSITION IN AGE GROUP.	3/54.		SCHOOL UNIFORM Regular.
ATTENDANCE	131/142.		PUNCTUALITY Ed. Q. 136. INTELLIGENCE QUOTIENT. 125

GENERAL REPORT has worked steadily and with interest, she has made gratifying progress. Her ~~English~~ Arithmetic is still her weak subject and she must make every effort to bring it up to the 120 mark.

F. R. Lamb Class Teacher

Age on 31. 12. 60 10 5/12 yrs. There has been a great improvement in arithmetic and she must keep up the rate of progress. The English grades are excellent.

R. Dillingham Head Teacher

Key to Grading: A—Specially Good B—Good C—Average D—Below Average E—Weak

Girl's report aged 10-11. Note the boys did Handwork and Gardening while the girls did Needlework.

In December 1960 Richard Dillingham wrote to the parents as follows: 'This term I am sending reports of those children who are in the two higher age groups. It is not possible for all children of the same age group to be in the same class, therefore the brighter children are in a class above, while a few retarded children may be in a class below the majority.

To compare the children in each age group I have given them standardised tests in English, Arithmetic, Reading and Spelling. The marks obtained from these tests enable us to find what national standard your child has reached in a particular subject. The marks are converted to quotients which take into account the age of the child. A quotient of 100 is average, one of 120 or over very good, one of 80 or under very weak.'

A subject quotient was obtained by dividing the subject age by the actual age and multipling by 100. Thus if a child's reading age was 10 years 5 months and the pupils actual age was 10 years 5 months then the quotient was 100.

Class teacher Miss Hawes and class, 1960s. During the mid-morning break monitors gave out free milk and straws. Each bottle contained a third of a pint. During the cold weather the milk often froze and pushed the silver foil top above the rim. The milk crates were then bought in and placed near the old stove in the classroom to thaw. Children thought it a great delight to suck the semi thawed milk through a straw.

Netball team, 1961.
Back row: Lesly Squires, Barbara Boutwood , Lesley Hyde, Mrs Joy.
Front row: Frances Bowers, Linda Janes, the Pay twins and Christine Lane.

Two 1960s classes with teachers Mrs Gravelle above and Mary Mountfort below.

Report by HM Inspectors

on Toddington Church of England Primary School, inspected 28, 29 and 30 June, 1961.

At the time of the last report in September 1952, 210 children attended this school,the main building of which was erected in 1854. There are now 351 pupils on the roll. Because of this rapid growth, and in spite of the addition of two not very satisfactory wooden huts on the restricted site, this old village school is no longer adequate. The provision of additional primary places in the area is now a matter of urgency. The Local Education Authority are anxious to provide better premises and have submitted proposals to which they give high priority, for inclusion in a building programme.

Teaching conditions are extremely difficult. The four infants' classes and one junior class are in the old school buildings, in rooms none of which is spacious and three of which are markedly deficient in size. The other four junior classes are in hutted classrooms with all the difficulties of heating by solid fuel stoves; it is reported that in winter the heating is very unsatisfactory. All the classrooms are difficult to ventilate. Although sanitary arrangements have been improved they remain deficient, both for children and for staff. There is no free space indoors, dinners are eaten in the classrooms and there can be no provision for an assembly, except outside in fine weather, for small additional teaching groups or for indoor physical activity. Since the opening of the London-Birmingham motorway, the road on which the school stands has become very busy. Access to the school by this route is dangerous and the classrooms which face the road are extremely noisy. The teaching staff, the domestic staff and the children are to be commended on the cheerfulness with which they make the best of these poor conditions.

The school garden is still a well-planned and useful addition to the site.

In the infants' classes the provision of equipment is seriously hampered by lack of storage space; even so it might be possible to provide more for number work and for creative activities. Except in the top two classes, there is need for many more books of the library type which may lead children to turn to reading for pleasure and for information. There are no easels in the school, so that painting is handicapped. With these exceptions, equipment generally is satisfactory, and the provision of small equipment is good.

The headteacher is an able organiser who has maintained high standards in what could be discouraging conditions. He is supported by a hard working staff who are on particularly good terms with the children. The school is notable for its air of industry and friendliness. If it should become possible to appoint an experienced teacher who could take some responsibility for leadership in the infants' classes, it would be to the school's advantage.

Religious instruction is based on the Surrey agreed syllabus, and is carefully given at all stages. Methodical teaching in the basic skills of reading, writing and arithmetic is carried out throughout the school. By the time the children leave, most can read with confidence and, especially in the top classes, they are encouraged to read widely. Some opportunities to use writing in interesting and purposeful ways are provided, but there might be a more systematic fostering of sustained independent writing on imaginative and informative topics. This could well be done in support of history and geography and nature study, of which useful but somewhat over-directed notes are made by the children. Arithmetical processes are well established and some useful measuring is performed, but there could be still more chances for the handling of quantities and measures in practical ways at all stages. Other mathematical ideas might be discussed from time to time.

Simple bookbinding and basketry are practised by the junior boys and raffia work and careful needlework by the girls. It might now be possible to introduce other materials and to encourage crafts of a less repetitive kind. Under a visiting teacher, valuable musical experiences are offered to the children, who not only sing well but enjoy listening. A vigorous programme of physical education is followed and there is excellent use of small equipment, especially under the guidance of the headmaster. It is good to record that the slower children of the third and fourth years are receiving particularly sympathetic and careful teaching.

The promise shown in the last report has been amply developed in spite of conditions which have become increasingly difficult with the growth of the school.'

School Football Team, 1961.
Pictured: Back row: Mr Dillingham, Aubrey Russell, Michael Bird, Stephen Petryszyn, Michael Brazier, Paul Tompkins.
Front row: Philip Stanghon, John Bryant, David Smith, Stephen Blackman, Ian Simmonds, John Stanley, Robert Edmonds.

October 1961, Old Peoples Luncheon with Annie Walker holding a pint glass while Queenie Bond and Beryl Hyde (both standing) look on.

Miss Walker taught at the National School for over 40 years. She was born in 1885 and started teaching at the age of 14 in 1899. My father, David Hart, was left handed and if she saw him writing with his left hand he got his knuckles rapped with a wooden ruler. My father's generation were forced to use their right hand at school. The word 'left' derives from the Anglo-Saxon word lyft *which means weak and the Latin word* sinistra *originally meant 'left', but later took on meanings of 'evil' or 'unlucky'.*

The admission registers show that boys who passed the 11-plus usually went to Luton Grammar School. However Nicky Pett was the first 1950s scholar to go to Dunstable Grammar School in 1956. By 1958 Dunstable Grammar School became the preferred school. The girls who passed normally went to Luton High School until 1961 when Queen Eleanor's School became first choice. Pupils who passed the 11-plus had a choice of grammar schools to go to. The single sex grammar schools, Dunstable Grammar School for boys and Queen Eleanor's Grammar School for girls, were the preferred choice because they obtained the best results.

The following is from *Chalk Dust and Boiled Cabbage* by Alan Scott :

'Critics of the 11-plus exam have described it as a 'modern miracle' because amazingly, each year the numbers of children who passed coincided exactly with the number of places available in a grammar school. Many maintained that such a result could have been achieved only by divine intervention!

The 11 plus exam itself was also something of a ritual ceremony. It was held on two days, several weeks apart. The first part was an intelligence test; for this each child was seated at a separate desk on the lid of which were two newly sharpened pencils and a clean sheet of the traditional pink blotting paper. When the children were seated a deathly hush prevailed as if in a court room when the jury is about to announce its verdict. The test booklets were distributed and names entered on the covers, then the command was given: "Open your booklets and begin." The test began with easy questions such as: Night is to day as black is to .....(white), socks are to feet as gloves are to ......(hands), hill is to high as valley is to .....(low). The questions gradually became more difficult and included mathematical and visual puzzles. After 40 or 45 minutes pencils were put down and the pupils went home to spend the remainder of the day as a holiday. The second part of the test was held about a month later when those children who passed the first test came back for another intelligence test, followed by arithmetic and English essay.'

BEDFORDSHIRE · COUNTY · COUNCIL
EDUCATION · COMMITTEE
SHIRE HALL · BEDFORD · TELEPHONE 67444

T · S · LUCKING · M·A · DIRECTOR · OF · EDUCATION
To whom all communications should be addressed

LWS/1/JMB 18 MAY 1961

Entrance to Secondary Grammar Schools, 1961.

Dear Sir/Madam,

I have pleasure in informing you that on the results shown in the County Assessment Tests the Education Committee will offer a place, tenable for so long as conduct and progress are satisfactory, to your daughter, , at Queen Eleanor's School, Dunstable. No tuition fees will be payable and books will be provided on loan throughout your daughter's school career.

It is generally desirable that pupils admitted to secondary grammar schools, which prepare children for the General Certificate of Education and other examinations, should remain until they are eighteen, but attendance for a minimum of five years of essential. Accordingly, if you wish to accept the place offered you will be required to keep your daughter at school for at least five years. If during the school course it should appear that another secondary school, e.g. a secondary technica or secondary modern school, would be more appropriate to your daughter's aptitudes, the possibility of transfer could be considered.

Particulars relating to the Authority's schemes for financial assistance are enclosed and if you wish to make an application, the slip attached to the accompanying letter should be completed and returned. The Education Committee will pay travelling expenses in the case of children who live more than three miles from the school.

If you wish to accept a place on the conditions outlined above, plea complete and return the attached form of acceptance and enclose your chil Birth Certificate, which will be returned to you in due course.

Yours faithfully,

Director of Education.

Parents were informed by letter of the 11-plus results. If a little brown envelope arrived it meant you had failed the exam while a nice big fat envelope containing additional information meant you had passed. I remember some of the girls crying at school because they had failed.

Passing the 11-plus was a mixed blessing. On the one hand it gave children from all backgrounds the chance to gain a worthwhile educational qualification and the opportunity of a career by studying for 'O' levels and if you wanted to take 'A' levels this might lead to university. On the other hand it was a huge departure point. It meant saying goodbye to friends that had not passed. A brand new uniform with a leather satchel and long trousers for the boys completed the transformation. It could take some time to adjust to changing classrooms for every lesson and carrying satchels loaded with books.

Mr Lamb's Class, July 1961, with his classroom pictured below (top right). The 'Nappy Wearers' and 'Greybeards' in the above picture include:

Back Row: Mary Mountfort, Tina Anderson , - , Lesly Squires, Margaret Pay, Susan Hoar , Catriona Cameron, Lesley Hyde, Linda Turney , Susan Walker, Cecelia Pay.

Third row: Standing: Corinne Pateman, - seated: Pauline Esteelle, Linda Horning, Linda Coles, - , -, Patricia Barnes, Mary Stanley, Joanna Harris, Ruth Weatherly, Isabel McClellan, Kathleen Holman.

Second Row (seated): Stephen Falberg, Philip Stanghon, Steven Petryszyn, Robert Cowper, Richard Peachey, John Bryant, Richard Hart, Norman Bates, John Stanley, Stephen Blackman.

Front row: Jennifer Lamb, David Smith, David Jamieson, Stephen Martin? Steven Bromwich Neville Lee, Sandra Clarke.

One pupil recalls that in her last year whilst in the huts, she and a group of some six other pupils locked the teacher outside the classroom. The key was thrown into the bushes. They were locked in and the teacher was locked out. It took the teacher ages to find the key. For this they were severely punished by Mr Dillingham. They were each given the slipper and made to stand outside the staff room during dinner time for a whole week. Physical discipline was a fact of life. Mr Lamb used to wrap your hand with the ring on his hand. Chalk was also thrown together with the occasional board rubber. The slipper was used for bad offenders.

Second Eleven Football Team, 1961.
Back row: Stephen Bromwich, - , David Newitt, Richard Hart, Stephen Falburg.
Front row: Michael Burrows, Patrick McLaughlin, Neville Lee, Robert Edmonds, Trevor Goble, Richard Hobbs, David Smith.

Yellows Football Team, 1962. Back row: - , Philip Fowler, Mr Lamb, Stephen Martin? Michael Walters.

Sitting on the ground are Patrick Mclaughlin and John Kitchiner. Teacher Mr Lamb taught Art amongst other subjects.

Class 1, July 1962. The teacher, Mr Lamb, taught the brightest children who were expected to pass the 11 plus. The class consisted of two different age groups, 9-10 and 10-11. The younger group were known as 'Nappy Wearers' and the older ones were 'Greybeards' After one year Nappy Wearers changed desks and were promoted to Greybeards but remained in the same class with a new bunch of Nappy Wearers. If you did not go into Mr Lamb's class you went into Mrs Gravelle's class.

Vehement opinions about his teaching methods still exist to this day. By 1967 Mr Lamb's class, which previously consisted of pupils from two different age groups, had become one age group. Christine Baker remembers the three tables in his L shaped classroom. 'The top table, placed near the teachers table consisted of pupils who were most likely to pass the 11 plus, the middle table consisted of pupils who might pass and the last table, placed near the toilets and practically out of sight of the blackboard, consisted of children who had no hope of passing.'

Mr Lamb had a vast fund of stories to keep everyone entertained. He could be strict but was regarded as fair. He managed to find nicknames for most of the class.

In September 1961 there were 308 children on the roll. There were 11 staff:

Mr R Dillingham (headmaster),
Mr F.R. Lamb (class 1 40 children)
Mrs C. Gravelle (class 2 38 children)
Mrs R. Joy (class 3a 39 children)
Mrs J. Williamson (class 3b 39 children)
Mr B. Deeley (music specialist ½ week)
Mrs D. Wootton (class 4 39 children)
Mrs M. Mountfort (class 5 41 children)
Mrs G. Cole (class 6 34 children)
Mrs D. Clark (class 7 38 children)
Miss S. Hawes (to take reception class in January)

Today the maximum class size would be 30 and a teacher would have helpers or classroom assistants.

George Hucklesby nicknamed 'Diggles' in action protecting school children walking along a muddy Conger path from Molly the cow. The children became frightened of the cattle that used to stand around the stile so a 'cow warden' was hired. 'Diggles' was appointed 'cow warden' on 10 July 1961 to 'escort the children across Conger path on which the cattle usually stand'. He was paid £2 3s 9d per week. Following the tragic death of pupil, Roy Goble in 1954, who was run down by a lorry in Station Road when returning home from school, it was decided to open up this footpath so that school children did not have to go to school along the busy road. Children could cross Station Road safely in December 1954 when Mr Pateman was appointed traffic warden to see the children safely across the road at the Post Office.

In 1962 'Diggles' appeared on the popular TV show What's My Line? *The chairman, Eammon Andrews (right) asked 'Diggles' to do a mime (waving on schoolchildren). The four panellists then had to work out exactly what George did for a living. They asked questions to which he replied either Yes or No. He beat the panel by answering No ten times and for many years his certificate hung in the Sow and Pigs. His occupation was described as cow warden. The nearest the panel got to his job title was that it had something to do with cattle.*

What's My Line?

Sunday 11 March 1962

What's My Line? was a BBC panel show in which TV host Eammon Andrews would invite a member of the public on stage and the panel had to guess their often unusual occupation after being shown a short mime. The panel of four could ask each guest questions relating to their work, subject to the discretion of the chairman. They couldn't ask 'What's your job?' Questions had to be asked which could only be answered yes or no. When the answer to a question was no the next panelist asked a question. That panelist continued to ask questions provided the guest answered yes. To beat the panel the guest had to truthfully answer no to 10 questions put by them. The panel won when they successfully guessed the occupation of the guest before the chairman had counted 10 'no' answers. The program had a celebrity guest on each week for whom the panelists had to cover their eyes.

Chairman: Eammon Andrews.

The Panel: David Nixon, Isobel Barnett, Barbara Kelly and Alan Melville.

Chairman: George William Hucklesby – A great name George. Where do you come from?
George: Toddington, Bedfordshire.
Chairman: Good. Will you give them a piece of mime?
(George mimes waving on schoolchildren).
Chairman: Alright. And if they get this one, well lets see. Coming up on your screen what George William Hucklesby does for a living:

He is a cow warden-He protects children from cows

Audience applauds.
Chairman: I can tell you that George is wage earning.
Panellist David Nixon starts the questioning:
Can I call you George-I forgot your other name-it's a long name. Do you work out of doors? –Yes.
Anything to do with agriculture? -No.
Chairman: Well very indirectly anyway.
Another panellist: May I call you George too? - Oui.
That part of Bedfordshire. Can I get rid of something? You are nothing at all to do with airships are you?- None.
Another Panellist: May I call you William. Agriculture is out but how about animals- George: Well yes.
It is nowhere near Whipsnade so we can take out the Zoo do we-completely?
George: Certainly.
They are nice ordinary animals that you would not be frightened to meet?
George: Well yes.
Is it one particular animal?- No.
A lot of animals?
Chairman: Well we'll give you a no for that anyway. It could have been yes. It depends how you meant the question. We'll give no. It could be several of one particular species.
Another Panellist: May I call you Mr Hucklesby? (audience laughs).

And it is one sex of one species. This sex whichever it is, has it got four legs.
George: Well have you known an animal without four legs.
Panellist: The Duck-Billed Platypus (laughter).
Are they sheep? - No.
Another panellist: Bigger than sheep?-Yes.
And its cows not bulls?
George: No it ain't.
And you do something with them cows?
Chairman: You're speaking aloud now.
Do you take them from place to place?- No.
Chairman: That's six gone.
Panellist: Do you say come home Nellie to all the cows?
Now the audience thought your occupation very funny. Can I leave out milk maid? –Yes
Do you touch the cows? Not at all-No.
Chairman: Seven gone.
Another panellist: Cows in Beds – Bedfordshire. Is the word cow that old fashioned Anglo Saxon word cow? Is it on the card?-Yes.
Good-We've got a Yes answer.
Cow something? - Yes.
Cow hand from a Bedfordshire Rio Grande! (laughter).
What can you do with cows if they don't move and your not a milkmaid?
George: That's for you to tell me (laughter)....
Panellist: Yes well it's very difficult George-your not sitting over here.
Panellist: Highly skilled-were you moving something on in your mime-anything?
Chairman: Yes I say you were.
I don't move anything.
Chairman: Yes quite right-No (laughter).
Panellist: The only other thing that cows have when they are about to be milked –they do better if they have music. Do you play music? No.

Chairman: You have beaten the panel. He was waving on schoolchildren. How do you come to have this particular job?
George: The mothers was frightened of the cows when the dogs run after them when they took the children to school so they reported it to the County Council and they said they must have a warden otherwise the children must go by the road and get knocked down by the lorries. So they had a warden to get the children across the field so they need not go on the road.
Chairman: Is it a very large herd of cows you protect the children from?
George: One cow.
(George whistles for his dog.)
Chairman: He is whistling up his mates. He wants to know the way to St Pancras, but someone will tell him.
(Applause).
Chairman: There is sometimes more than one cow. There is one at the moment and it is a very dangerous cow.

Football Team, 1963. Back row: - , Charlie Rogers, Mrs Joy, - , Philip Fowler. Front row: -, Barry Cooper, Jimmy Aries, Raymond Baker, Robert Swain, Paul Hyde, Colin Battams.

Class 3, May 1964. Christian names only apart from two:
Back row : Stephen, Jennifer, Paul, Maria, Kenneth, Peter, Brett Jones.
3rd row: Robert, Mandy, Leonard, Rosalyn, Adrian, Anne, Paul Hyde, Patricia.
2nd row: Diane, Brian, Fiona, Ian, Patricia, Nigel, Joy, Edward, Susan.
Front row: Malcolm, Julia, Patricia, Katherine, Anne, Christine, Lesley, Philip.

Mrs Joy's retirement, 9 April 1965. She taught for 41 years at the school and had some 2,250 children in her charge during that time. Headteacher Mr Dillingham said 'she had a genuine love for her work and had striven to find virtue in every child. Her reliability had made my task as headmaster an easy one.' Pictured above is the school choir which was directed by Mr Deeley. Mrs Joy was given a silver tea service as a retirement present.

Mrs Joy began her career when the standard cure for writing with your left hand was a smart rap on the knuckles with a heavy wooden ruler.

At the top of each desk was a groove to rest the pen or pencil. On the right of each half was a circular hole for the earthenware ink pot. A liftable lid meant that exercise books and text books could be kept in the desk. At the start of each term each child found on their desk a new pencil, a penholder with a shiny nib, a foot rule, a full ink pot and a sheet of blotting paper. The blotting paper was used to dry ink when a page in the exercise book had to be turned, to mop up the all too frequent blots, and also as a rest for the non-writing hand, thus keeping the work clean and tidy.

Miss Troubridge's class, about 1960s. Pupils pictured include:
Back row: Ian Darby, - , - , - , - , Karen Baker. Class teacher Miss Troubridge.
Third row: - , Gary Saunders, Gary Hoar, Jonathan Perry, Jill Smith, Elaine Buckingham, - , Linda Klimas, Ralph Harper, - .
Second row: - , - , - , Ian Jones, - , - , Leonard Hull -, -, -.
Front row: John Fossey, - , Roland Alderson, - , Marion White, - , - , Robert Green.

Mrs Fern's class 2b, June 1966.
Back row: Stephen Byron, - , - , Janice Shaw, Tina Brightman, - , Kathleen Jenkins?, Trevor Cook, - , Susan Curl? Mark Whinnett.
Middle row: Lindsay Claridge, - , Lyn Stringer, Julie Barker, Christine Hart, Sharon McLaughlin, - , Daphne Chalmers , Susan Philips , Lesley Windmill.
Front row: Graham Coles, Stephen King, Clive Goodship, - , - , Melvyn Bryant, -

Audience at prize giving listening to Denis Hyde speaking as Chairman of the Governors saying goodbye to the old school, July 1967. He stated that during its 113 year existence, the school had only four headmasters, the first Mr Billingham, the second Mr Thomas, Mr Wootton and the present headmaster Mr R. Dillingham. The move to a new school meant that all the pupils could again be housed under one roof. Because of the increase in numbers the infants had been going to Station Road and the juniors to Leighton Road.

Going home time on the last day. A handful of parents wait outside Toddington Primary School, Station Road, for their children, July 1967. In those days most children made their own way home unlike today where the majority of children are dropped off and picked up by their parents. This can cause problems with traffic congestion and parking.

The following is a list taken from the School Log Book which was printed in the *National School Centenary* in 1954 with comments by Richard Dillingham:

The first pupil:

Mr H. C. Russell has in his possession a photograph of a lady who claimed to be the first scholar to be admitted. She was Mrs. Tilcock (whose maiden name was Mary Ann Barbey). On the first day the school opened, Mr. Barbey took Mary down and a queue formed at the entrance. When the door opened there was a rush and Mr. Barbey carried his daughter to be first in. At first fees were charged for tuition.

1865. Lowered the school fees from two pence to a penny for labourers' children.

1865. Being Shrove Tuesday, according to ancient custom, the children have a half holiday. (All this in addition to the normal holiday periods amounting to 10 weeks.)

School Treats are always an incentive to good attendances.

1868. (July 20th) Told the children this morning, there would be a treat and that the tickets will be given out this week – a good school in consequence. Indeed one boy whose mother said he was not coming this week, has this afternoon, made his appearance.

1872. The school fees rose this week and this has told slightly on the attendance.

1872. One poor lad at school without a jacket. Told the boy to tell his parent to let him wear a pinafore or jacket and told him I should be sorry to have to send him home if he came in his shirt sleeves again.

1877. All children above seven paying 3d. each.

1877. A child's book was taken from the lobby by some roguish stranger.

1878. I caused a pail of water, a scrubbing brush, a flannel, some soap and a towel to be brought into the room this morning and made some dirty boys wash themselves before the others.

1878. A mother entered the school and took her child away. The woman, who misbehaved herself last week, has since been to the school and apologised, preferring to do this than going to Woburn Court.

That there was intense rivalry between the National School and Wesleyan School is evident from the following entry:

> I have learned today through some of the parents that their children have been decoyed away to the Wesleyan School, in consequence of their committee offering to pay their fees - they not being able to get our children in any other way and having just engaged the fourth Master since March and are now going to make a spurt to beat or defeat this school.

1878. There are a great many fees in arrears, but we cannot press the payments of them too much as many of the parents are out of work and have been so for some time.

1878. Two children sent to school both under three were sent home till such time as they should be three.

The education act of 1870 made education compulsory and it was not surprising that this was not popular with some.

1878. Some of the forced children are getting both irregular and troublesome, only coming to school when obliged.

1880. (5th July). The attendance somewhat decreased owing to the Board of Guardians having issued an order allowing all children above the age of eight to go on farm work.

However, the children were often permitted to go to work and the task of getting any continuity in the school work must have been most difficult.

1881. (15th July). School gradually thinning as the children are engaged in carrying dinners to fathers making hay etc. Whoever built the school must have intended it to last at least a century. It is a pity that as time went on adequate money could not be raised to its proper maintenance. It must have originally been lit with oil lamps for there is an entry in 1863 that the gas fitters were in the school. These gas fittings were not removed until 1951 when the school was redecorated and more electric lights put in. In 1890 was recommended that increased lobby accommodation should be provided so as to avoid necessity of hanging cloaks and caps in the rooms.

1883. (November 5th) I had to go to the Town and send the boys down to the school.

1884. The fees are lower than they should be owing to the great scarcity of work in the parish. Many parents have done no work for some weeks. The children in consequence are badly fed and this affects their work.

1885. T.G. excused school on account of want of sharpness.

1885. I admitted three children by the name of B, from the hamlet of Chalton. They were of the ages of 9, 7 and 5 do not seem to have been in a day school before.

1886. (10th of Nov.) Some of the fathers will have no regular work from now till March 1887. These parents earn some weeks 2s. and this has to support the family. These children cannot possibly pay any fee. I have written the above because I have lately taken a few test cases as I do occasionally and find that some of the poor children come to school absolutely without breakfast during the winter months, badly clothed and scarcely shod at all.
(At first children were permitted to come to school when three years old and some tried to send the children before.)

1887. Last Friday week, a parent was fined 5s. including costs, his boy being absent 139 times out of a possible 139, the parent having employed the boy who was able to earn 5s weekly. The parent has shown his idea of the punishment by continuing to employ the boy.

1887. F.K. a lad, who attended school regularly through the year has lately become deaf, dumb, blind and subject to fits in turns - through excitement in attending the Salvation Army meeting.

1889. The men of the town being employed as navvies on the "line", the farmers are employing boys for hay work.

1889. A child is having difficulty with her sum, her teacher told her to go stay behind at 4pm and try. The child immediately put herself into a passionate temper and cried for over one and a half hours. What can I do in such a case?

1890. The Rector told me this morning that he should object to the school being used in the Children's Annual Concert, (object to buy prizes and certificates), if Red Riding Hood was performed or anything with any characters in it.

1891. I have placed a set of desks in the Gallery for Std. I.

1892. On Monday last, we admitted ten fresh children who are boarded out in Toddington from Islington Parish. They are well conducted children.

1892. I yesterday sent 11s to the Lord Mayor's fund for the relief of the sufferers by the terrible loss of H.M.S. Victoria - the humble but cheerful and sympathetic contribution of the staff and scholars of the National School.

1895. After a Magic Lantern Entertainment in the evening, I have found:
(1) Irons of two desks broken.
(2) A quantity of oil spilt on the floor.
(3) The bottom and roller torn off Clause VII.
I have never before known such things to happen.

1896. A Stag Hunt Party was passing through the town, the whole of the senior boys as was only natural went off. The school therefore did not meet in the afternoon of yesterday.

1896. It is pointed out by the Inspector that the number of offices is quite insufficient for the number of girls and infants in attendance. The playground must be put in order. (The playground and walls have always been a drain on the funds.)

1897. The managers drew a cheque for £32 10s. for a new brick wall. About £28 of this has been raised by the staff.

1899. The boys are very keen on the War News.

1900. (March) Yesterday morning when we received the copy of the telegram saying that Ladysmith was relieved the children were in the playground. Their joy knew no bounds - they jumped and danced about, shouting and cheering and throwing up their caps. We marshalled them all into school, soon got out our Union Jack and then marched to the Green. We sang patriotic songs, the National Anthem and gave them [three] cheers for all the Generals connected with the war and for the rank and file of the Army and Navy and for her Gracious Majesty, Queen Victoria. The rest of the day was a holiday.

1901. (April 23rd) This day was received from Messrs. Malcolm & Sons the fine school organ - a gift to the Day & Sunday Schools from the ladies of the Guild.

1901. Many of the parents of the elder boys are asking if their lads can go to work for a few weeks. As the children, as a rule, attend remarkably well during the greater part of the year, I tell the parents to use their own discretion. The money the boys earn helps to clothe them in the winter.

1902. I have gone to the Town Pond at 9am and 1:30pm each day and rang the children off the ice.

1902. (June 2nd) Peace proclaimed. All our school flags were got out, the girls soon got large boughs of May blossom and bedecked themselves and we all marched up the town. The Rector (Chairman of the Managers) and Dr Waugh (correspondent) met us on the Green. The Rector made a patriotic speech, Rule Britannia and The King were sung and hearty cheers given.

On June 20th there was a grand parade and June 23rd a Coronation holiday.

1903. June 1903 seems to have been similar to June of 1953, for Mr Thomas records that four fires were needed all one week because it was so cold and wet and that it rained continuously for over 60 hours.

1904. The Parish Council have written complaining of the boys' ball for getting kicked over into the Cemetery.

1905. (Feb. 24th) Black Friday. On February 24th, 1905, Mr. Thomas heads his entry Black Friday. This has indeed been a black letter day. We have news this morning that our three King's Scholarship Candidates had all failed. We received what we consider a most unjust report from the Diocesan Inspector who seems to have marked the school 'Very Fair' because the scholars did not answer their questions on the Confirmation Service. The usual mark of the School has been 'Excellent'.

We have had two little girls, quarrelling going home and thus upset their parents.

1905. This morning while the elder scholars were having a lesson on General Information. D. Havilland came in and stayed and listened the whole time.

1907. The H.M.I. has ordered that the boys have to play in the playground and not in the road.

1907. 28 boys and girls have been given a basin of hot soup before they leave school at noon. 89 are given hot milk with bread and sugar before work begins in the morning.

1907. The American organ used in the Day School is the property of the Sunday School, Rev J.C.C. Pipon.

1910. King Edward VII died. Most of the children are wearing some sign of mourning.

1911. In measuring and weighing the children, though no notice was given to the children that they would be required to take their boots off there was only one instance of a scholar with unmended untidy stockings. This out of 30 children speaks volumes for Toddington parents.

1911. (July 28th). On Monday about 90 children were absent. They got up at 3 a.m. and went to various vantage spots to see if any of the aeroplanes taking part in the great race could be seen. Ten of the machines were visible. Two came to grief in sight of Toddington folks, one at Streatley and one at Barton. A rush was made across the valley to Streatley.

1912. Diocesan Inspection. The Inspector - a strange gentleman was exceedingly pleasant in his manner.

1913. A huge balloon passed over the school yesterday at 4 p.m. just as the children were being dismissed. (I am sure the appearance of a huge balloon over the school in November 1953 caused as much excitement as the one 40 years before).

1914. Girls knitting socks and scarves for the soldiers.

1914. Infant department to be a separate school under Miss Blower.

1915. Walter Hobbs received a bible for 11 years perfect attendance.

1917. Water ran down the north wall in streams.

1917. There is an influx of children from the London area on account of the incessant air raids.

1918. H.T. played truant this morning, visiting an aeroplane which had descended in a field near the school. Debarred from play for a week.

1920. The Temperature of the big room at 9 o'clock was 28° at 10.30 was only 34°. The children were kept moving as much as possible, but it was often too cold for written work.

1924. The children had an opportunity of hearing the King's Speech on St. George's Day through the kindness of Mrs. Ashley Pope who lent her wireless set.

1938. Workmen have removed parts of the floor in and near the 'gallery' cupboard where mushroom growths appeared before the holiday.

1938. (Sept. 28th). Consequent upon the grave developments in Europe and the threat of war I have received notice that A.R.P. officials will visit the school and fit gas masks. Also instructions as to what to do if a state of emergency is declared.

1939. (Sept. 3rd). Many women and young children evacuated from London arrived.

1940. (July 26th) 152 children arrived in Toddington. I was billeting officer. The junior part of school is to be on half time.

1940. (July 26th). Muslin put in the windows and other windows bricked up for shelters.

1940. (Nov. 6th). Several bombs dropped in Long Lane.

1943. (May 21st). Wings for Victory Week. We raised £187.10s.

1945. (May 9th). VE Day. The school closed.

1947. (Feb. 22nd). Nine radiators burst in the great freeze up. School closed for two months.

1951. (May 22nd) A party of children were taken round the Church by the Rector, the Rev. F. W. Hunt.

1951. (May 24th) We received the news that the Rector had died in his sleep during the night. This came as a great shock as he seemed perfectly well and cheerful when he showed us the church.

1952. (February 6th). News was received of the death of King George VI. The flag was flown at half mast and the football match arranged for the evening cancelled.
On February 15th, a memorial service to his late Majesty was held in the school.

1953. (June 2nd). The Coronation of Her Majesty Queen Elizabeth II. After a Fancy Dress Parade some of the scholars gave a Country Dancing display on the Green.

Spectators on the Green watch the Country Dancing display. Wendy Shepherd (nearest to camera) and Suzanne Clifford were among the dancers.

Teachers at National and Primary School

1864 William Rapsey, assisted by pupil teacher Henry Wildman.

1865 Edwin Billingham assisted by pupil teachers William Heathcote, William Spring and Elizabeth Carr.

1875 Charles Thomas (headteacher) with pupil teachers H.G. Abbiss, E. Osborn, E. Carr and M. Muckleston who was monitor. Miss Muckleston started as a monitor and progressed to become a teacher. She never left the school!

1887 Charles Thomas (headteacher), Gertrude Abbiss, (certified teacher), Maria Muckleston (assistant teacher), and pupil teachers Emily Whinnet, Annie Horley, Annie Harris, Ada Seymour and Annie Joy.

1896 Charles Thomas (headteacher), Alice Hillman, Maria Muckleston, Sarah Briden, CG Thomas, May Muckleston, and candidates Albert Smith, George Hart.

1900 Charles Thomas (headteacher), Margaret Shepherd, Maria Mucklestone, George Parien Hart who were assistants. Ellen Smith, Flora Clark, Margaret Thomas, Laura Horley, Bertha Evans and Annie Walker.

1917 B.M. Wootton, (headteacher), (TC) salary £110, Miss M. Muckleston (U) salary £65, Miss E.K. Neale (U) salary £55, Elizabeth Hobbs caretaker £16.10s (£16.50).

1922 B.M. Wootton (headteacher), Maria Muckleson, Mary Elizabeth Higgs, Mabel Elizabeth Hobbs, Rosetta Ellen Deal, Mrs Cole, Miss Annie Walker.

1948 B.M. Wootton (headteacher), Miss R Dreyheller Ashcroft, Mrs D.M. Wootton, Mr K.C. Briggs, Mrs L.E. Pett, Mrs R.E. Lang-Sadler and Mrs M.R. Mountfort.

1954 Mr R. Dillingham (headteacher), Mrs R. Joy, Mrs R.E. Lang-Sadler, Mr F.R. Lamb, Mr A.F. Brooker, Mrs D.M. Wootton, Miss E.O.W. Troubridge, Mrs R. Wegener (music) and Mrs A. Shepherd (caretaker).

1961 Mr R. Dillingham (headteacher), Mr F.R. Lamb, Mrs C. Gravelle, Mrs R. Joy, Mrs J. Williamson, Mrs D. Wootton, Mrs M. Mountfort, Mrs G. Cole, Mrs D. Clark, Miss Hawes and Mr B. Deeley (music).

William Hyde Awards

The Toddington Old Boys Association funds the William Hyde Awards named after its founder chairman, which are presented annually to four young people at Parkfields School. The Association prize for those who would make the best citizens is a very coveted one, and is open to all pupils. Below is a list of the recipients from 1945 to 1963 when two prizes were given to the Voluntary Primary School and another two to the County Secondary Modern School.

	Primary School		Secondary School	
1945	Mavis Smith	Roger Turner	Dorothy Simmonds	Peter Coles
1946	Jean Roberts	John Smith	Irene Neale	Geoffrey Leary
1947	No award, owing to re-organisation of schools		Jean Leary	Thomas Claridge
1948	No award, owing to re-organisation of schools		Margaret Kingham	Geoffrey Rowe
1949	Ann Morgan	Peter Caldecourt	Margaret Rowe	Frederick Neale
1950	Christine Deary	James Wooliscroft	Jean Allen	Alfred Dudley
1951	Mary Pateman	William Wright	Hilary Chapman	Derek Buckingham
1952	Peter Muckleston	Rosalie Hancox	Anne Rowe	Kenneth Itzinger
1953	Susan Marlow	Malcolm Fleet-Chapman	June Kempton	James McGowan
1954	John Pett	Rona Kitchiner	Jean Wilson	Anthony Ball
1955	Roger Fox	Judith Oliver	Brian Chapman	Daphne Odell
1956	Colin Osborn	Susan Nicholls	Valerie Cleaver	John Hanson
1957	Colin Nash	Jennifer Parrott	David Cooper	Margaret Cook
1958	Arthur Johnson	Mary Coles	John Oliver	Judith Oliver
1959	Christopher Day	Heather Pears	Sheila Odell	Philip Emerton
1960	Peter Smith	Margaret Conquest	Vilma Wilson	Sonnie Wing
1961	Stephen Blackman	Lesley Hyde	Linda Heeps	Richard Fox
1962	David Smith	Catherine Ward	Jennie Fish	Jeffrey Collett
1963	Raymond Baker	Rosemary Baker	Ann Neal	Paul Wilson

National and Primary School Pupils

Pupils admitted between 1917 and 1961 to the National/Primary School

Acutt Ivy
Acutt Winifred M
Adams Olive
Affleck John J
Ahern Anthony N L
Aird Rose
Alcorn Valerie L
Aldred Alan S
Aldred Aubrey
Aldred Dorothy
Aldred John
Aldred Lesley R
Aldred Michael
Aldred Pauline W
Aldred Philip E
Aldred Robert
Aldred Robert S
Allen Betty
Allen Douglas G
Allen Freda B
Allen Jack
Allen Jean
Allen Jean C
Allen June L
Allen Peter L
Allen Roy E J
Allen William H
Alsford Ronald
Alsford Stanley
Anderson Barbara
Anderson Christina F
Anderson L
Anderson Margaret E
Anderson Susan J
Andrews Michael
Anker David S
Anker Mark
Ansell Derek Chas
Ansell Donald
Ansell Elsie I
Ansell Evelyn
Ansell Frederick J
Ansell Gwendolen E
Ansell Hilda F
Ansell Ivy
Ansell Laura
Ansell Phyllis
Ansell Robert
Answell Howard
Appleton Iris D
Archer Wilfred M
Aries James M
Armstrong Christopher J
Arnold Graham C
Arnold Patricia A
Arnold Richard D

Asbridge Michael V
Ashby Hazel L
Ashby Jessie P
Ashby Vera
Ashby Winifred
Aston Peter
Aston Stanley F
Atkins Audrey
Atkins Georgina I
Atkinson Bert
Atkinson Christopher H
Atkinson Ellen
Atkinson Eric
Atkinson Fred
Atkinson Henry
Atkinson Lily
Atkinson Sheila
Atthews Eric
Atthews Rita
Atzema Maeve J
Austen Linda D
Austin Carol
Avery Dorothy J
Ayres Doris
Ayres Freda
Ayres Ivy
Ayres John C
Ayres Leonard G
Ayres Patience
Ayres Wendy
Babister Shirley M
Bailey Annette C
Bailey Dawn
Bailey Jennifer
Bailey Lorraine
Bainton David H
Bainton Kathleen
Bainton Peter
Bainton Stella M
Baker Alice L
Baker Arthur
Baker Aubrey A B
Baker Audrey V
Baker Brian C
Baker Charles T
Baker Daphne E M
Baker Derek
Baker Dorothy
Baker Douglas
Baker Edward
Baker George H
Baker George R
Baker Gwendoline M
Baker Hildreth
Baker Jane
Baker John W

Baker Joy M
Baker Kenneth J
Baker Margaret G M
Baker Pamela R
Baker Raymond J
Baker Rosemary G
Baker Stephen W
Ball Anthony C
Ball Robert F
Ballard Fred
Bandy Joan E
Banks Garrard C
Barnes Glenys E
Barnes Helen R
Barnes Janet
Barnes Patricia F
Barrow Brian
Bartlett Janet
Bates Arthur F
Bates Dorothy
Bates Dorothy
Bates Edna M
Bates Evelyn
Bates Judith C
Bates Marjorie
Bates Mary
Bates Norman C
Bates Richard A
Bates Rita M
Bates Stella
Bates William H
Battams Colin
Battams Graham R
Battams Patricia E
Battams Pauline
Baumber Lorraine C
Baumber Vivian O
Beckett Paul G
Beeton Greville A
Bell Elaine D
Bell Ronald E
Bernstein Edelle S
Berry Alison
Berry Christopher C
Biddlecombe H
Biddlecombe R
Biddulph Amy S
Bierton Kathleen I
Bierton Walter C
Biggs James A
Bignell Kathleen
Billington Alb.
Billington Don I
Billington Leonard R
Billington Stan
Billington Victor

Bird Michael S P
Blackman Barabara
Blackman Edith
Blackman James
Blackman Linda M
Blackman Peggy
Blackman Stephen J
Blackmore John H
Blackmore June
Blackmore Margaret
Bland Ernest
Bland Ellen
Bland George
Bland Robert W
Bland Rosemary A
Bleaney Eric M
Bleaney Stephen L
Bloomer Pamela
Bloomer Paul
Bloomer Paul B
Bodsworth Dorothy
Boffey James A
Boffey Helen S
Bolter Dorothy
Bolter Eleanor
Bolter Henry W
Bone Peter W
Bone Terence J
Bonner Dorothy M
Bonner Ernest
Bonner Frederick
Bonner Gwendolen L
Bonner Irene
Bonner Maureen J
Bonner Michael J
Bosson Simone
Bosson Teresa
Boutwood Barbara M
Boutwood Cynthia
Boutwood Joy D
Bowers Alan
Bowers Florence J
Bowers Frances
Bowers George
Bowers Harry
Bowers Janet
Bowers John
Bowers Joy
Bowers Lorna
Bowers Michael D
Bowers Nicholas J
Bowers Terence
Bowler Jean
Boxford Leslie Cyril
Brake Jack
Branch David

Brand Brian A
Brand Carol M
Brand Desmond I W
Brand Edgar T
Brand Ivor D H
Brand Jane
Brand Joy B
Brand Lawrence D
Brand Lorna R
Brand Michael J
Brandom Ethel
Brandom Margaret
Brandom Rose
Bray Mark C
Brazier Arthur F
Brazier Catherine E
Brazier Dorothy
Brazier Gwendolen
Brazier Ivy G
Brazier Kenneth
Brazier Leonard A
Brazier Leslie
Brazier Margaret L
Brazier Mary A
Brazier Michael H
Brazier Nancy
Brazier Robert
Brazier Robert H
Brazier Russell H
Brazier Violet
Breed Francis W J
Breed William
Brewer Annie
Brewer Evelyn M
Brewer George
Brewer Jack
Brewer Jacqueline M
Brewer Joy L
Brewer Maurice J
Brewer Pearl
Brewer Philip
Brewer Robin D
Brewer Sarah
Briden Arthur S
Briden Dan
Briden Horace
Briden Ronald
Brigginshaw Bernard F
Briggs Robert G
Bright Connie
Bright Edward
Bright George
Brinklow Eric G
Brinklow Lawrence
Brinklow Marjorie
Brinklow Rex W
Brittain Dorothy
Brittain Eileen
Brommich Stephen J
Bromwich Gary C
Brooke Jacqueline
Brooker Christine
Brookson Patricia
Broom Avril N
Brown Albert
Brown Barbara
Brown Brenda M
Brown Carol Eunice
Brown Carol S
Brown Charles
Brown David
Brown Edna
Brown Eric I
Brown Frances E
Brown G Trevor
Brown Gibson L
Brown Howard R
Brown Iris E M
Brown Ivy or Joy
Brown Jacqueline L
Brown Keith A
Brown Lestral I
Brown Lily
Brown Mary
Brown Mary F
Brown Myrtle
Brown Nancy
Brown Peter D
Brown Phyllis M
Brown Raymond G
Brown Robin
Brown Ronald
Brown Sandra V
Brown Terence
Brown Tom
Brown Trevor J
Brown Valerie M
Brown Victor
Brown Winifred
Bryan Arthur G
Bryan Ronald
Bryant Derek
Bryant George H
Bryant John E
Bryant Margaret
Bryant Margaret E
Bryant Paul M
Bryant Peter C
Bryant Peter R
Bryant Richard W
Bryson Colin
Bryson Peter
Buchan Dennis
Buchan Patricia
Buckingham Ann E
Buckingham Aubrey P
Buckingham Aubrey R
Buckingham Avis J
Buckingham Barry J
Buckingham Brian
Buckingham David Y
Buckingham Derek C
Buckingham Dora
Buckingham Doreen N
Buckingham Edward J
Buckingham Enid
Buckingham Eva
Buckingham Evelyn
Buckingham Frances
Buckingham Fred
Buckingham Grace
Buckingham J
Buckingham Jacqueline
Buckingham Janet M
Buckingham Jean I
Buckingham Kathleen M
Buckingham Margaret E
Buckingham May
Buckingham Pamela J
Buckingham Pauline E
Buckingham Philip
Buckingham Phyllis
Buckingham Raymond
Buckingham Rita
Buckingham Stephen
Buckingham Stewart
Buckingham Susan
Buckingham Suzanne M
Buckingham Thelma R
Buckingham Violet
Buckman Norman R
Buda David M
Buda Marylin I
Bull Doreen
Bull Walter D S
Bullen Elizabeth
Bullen Ivy
Bullen May F
Bullen Robert
Bullock Brenda
Bunning Frank E
Bunning Rita M
Bunning Ronald G
Burch Christine M
Burch Valerie M
Burden James
Burgess Adrian
Burgess Bryan
Burgess Ivan R W
Burgess Lionel
Burgin Denis
Burgin John H
Burman Graham
Burman Leonard G
Burman Robin B
Burman Rodney M
Burn Gary
Burrows Michael G
Burrows Richard J
Butcher Janet
Butler Letty
Butters Hazel I
Butters William B
Bye Frederick
Byrne Ivy E
Cain Eileen
Cain Maureen
Caldecourt Barbara
Caldecourt David J
Caldecourt Eric
Caldecourt Peter V
Cameron Alison C
Cameron Catriona J
Cantle Cherolyn S R
Cantle Francis L
Capell Victor E
Carlin Anita M
Carlin Janet
Carney Joseph
Carney Reginald
Carney Robert
Carpenter Dorothy
Carpenter Edith E
Carpenter Elizabeth
Carpenter Janet
Carpenter John
Carpenter William
Carr Madge
Carr Patricia
Carr Robert
Carter Dorothy
Carter Douglas P
Carter Lilian R
Carter William A
Catling Alec
Cattermole Ronald
Cawley Brian
Cawley Jonathan
Chadburn Evelyn
Chalmers Daphne
Chalmers George A
Chalmers Ian
Chance David
Chance Kathleen A
Chance Kenneth F
Chance Maida I
Chance Norris
Chance Pauline
Chance Sylvia I P
Chandler Jennifer A
Chapman Agnes
Chapman Bernice
Chapman Percy
Chapman Percy
Chapman Stewart G
Chapman Susan
Chapman Terry
Chapple David
Chapple Diane
Chelley Jennifer A
Childs Audrey C
Childs Alan
Childs Derrick
Childs Frederick H

Childs Mary
Childs Mary M
Childs Patricia R
Childs Phyllis B
Childs Richard J
Church Donald H
Claridge Charles W
Claridge Lindsay
Claridge Terence P
Claridge Thomas
Clark Brian
Clark Brian P
Clark Constance V
Clark Denise
Clark Julia A
Clark Leslie J
Clark Michael J
Clark Stanley
Clark Stanley V
Clark Stephen P
Clark William
Clarke Angela W
Clarke Aubrey
Clarke Beatrice
Clarke Charles
Clarke Dora
Clarke Dora
Clarke Ella
Clarke Howard W
Clarke Sandra E
Clarke Stella
Clarke Stella I
Clarke Vera
Cleaver Ivy
Cleaver Valerie L
Clifford Anne
Clifford Edna
Clifford Gwen S
Clifford Suzanne
Cobb Phyllis L A
Cobb William E
Cockings William A
Coe Albert W
Coe Kathleen
Coe William C
Cole Christopher
Cole Philip J
Coleman Barbara L
Coles Alison M J
Coles Betty
Coles David
Coles David E
Coles Doreen M
Coles Graham
Coles Linda J
Coles M
Coles Mary W
Coles Maurice S
Coles Paul
Coles Sidney
Coles Stanley
Coles Trevor G
Coles William S D
Collett Jeffery W
Collinson Ann E
Coman Beatrice M
Compton Peter B
Conquest Janet
Conquest Margaret
Conquest Stephen
Conway Lesley
Conway Stephen P
Cook Elsie L
Cook Harry
Cook Ian N
Cook Iris
Cook Jennifer S
Cook Nicholas
Cook Ronald
Cook Susan I
Cooke David G
Cooke Jennifer M
Cooke John
Cooke Margaret
Cooke Patricia A
Cooke Richard
Cooke Richard L
Cooper Aubrey E
Cooper Barry E
Cooper David
Cooper Leonard F
Cooper Sandra D
Cornwall Margaret A
Cossons Joan
Cossons Ronald
Costin Norman B
Costin Roger C
Cotier Jean
Cotier Jean E
Cottle Shirley
Cotton Alfred
Cotton Charles
Cotton Thomas
Courtenay Anthony L
Cowan Agnes
Cowley Christine
Cowper Malcolm
Cowper Robert A
Cowper Roger
Cox Anthony H
Cox George
Cox Margaret
Cox Sharman E
Crawley Jospeh
Crees Diane
Cripps Dorothy
Cripps Irene
Cripps Stanley
Crisp Ronald
Crosby Andrew
Crosby James
Crosby Timothy R J
Cross Grace L
Crother Sally E
Cumberland Eileen L G
Cumberland Joyce M
Curtis Anne
Curtis Francis
Curtis Isobel S
Curtis John H S
Curtis Mary A
Curzon Kester
Curzon Peter J
Curzon Quentin
Curzon Terence
Cutting Cyril
Cutting James
Danes Eva M
David John H
Davies Betty F
Davies Zena
Davis Brian
Davis Leslie R
Davis Margaret
Dawes Pamela
Dawson Gordon S
Day Christopher R
Day George R
Day Lucy
Day Stuart P
Day Susan M
Day Violet
Dayman Christopher E
Dayton George S
Dayton Una
Deary Christine
Deary Peter J
Deering Bernard G
Deering Sheila M
Dell Malcolm
Denmark Alan J
Denmark Hedley
Dennis Jeffrey A
Denton Dorothy E
Denton Edith
Denton Hazel
Denton Mary D
Denton Rita
Denton Walter
Derry Philip
Dillingham Christine
Dillingham Margaret K
Dix Clifford
Dixon Edith E
Dixon Joyce
Dodson Beryl
Dodson Claud
Dodson May
Dodson Reginald
Dodson William C H
Doubleday Jean
Downer Fred
Downing Sandra
Draper Alice S
Draper Elizabeth M
Dudley Alfred W
Dudley Margaret A
Duncan Julia A
Duncan Teresa Louise
Dunford Patricia A
Dunkley Stanley
Dunn Sandra P
Dunn Stanley G
Dunne Betty E
Dunne David
Dunne Peter
Dunnell Graham A
Dunning Walter
Dunsdon Denis
Dunstone Robert
Dyer Diana A
Dyer Geoffrey
Dyer Harry
Dyer Ivy
Dyer Maureen L
Dyer Phyllis R
Eaton Joan
Eaton Winifred
Eddolls Robert W
Edge John
Edmonds Martin D
Edmonds Paul R
Edmonds Robert W
Edmonds Stephen
Edwards Alan T
Edwards Beverley J
Edwards Carol A
Edwards Elaine
Edwards Eric F
Edwards James
Edwards June M
Edwards Martin P
Edwards Melvyn J
Edwards Shirley A
Elliott Cheryl A
Elliott Hugh
Elliott Karen
Elliott Peter
Ellis Charlotte M
Ellis Comfort
Ellis Lavinia
Ellis Martha
Ellis Susan H
Elvin Beverley
Elvin David
Emery David G
England Carl
Errington Albert
Errington Graham
Estalle Pauline
Evans Bertie
Evans Beryl J
Evans Daisy
Evans Deanne

Evans Donald
Evans Donovan
Evans Edna M
Evans James W
Evans Jane E
Evans Lily
Evans Percy
Evans Peter E
Evans Peter Ronald
Evans Sidney
Everitt Bernard
Everitt Cyril
Everitt Dennis
Fairbairn Patricia A
Falberg Hazel
Falberg Nigel P
Falberg Stephen C G
Farmer Joyce
Farmer Patricia
Farwell Penelope A
Fay Linda H
Fellowes Susan
Fellowes Terence
Fenlon Susan A
Feskew Maria
Field Ann
Field Mary
Field Paul A
Finch Howard
Finch Stuart F
Finnis Jean
Fisher Millie
Fleckney Austin
Fleckney Margaret
Fleet-Chapman Bryan G
Fleet-Chapman Judy A
Fleet-Chapman Malcolm
Fletcher Arthur Alex
Fletcher Audrey K
Fletcher Daphne
Fletcher Harold
Fletcher Harold R
Fletcher Howard C R
Fletcher Jane
Fletcher Joyce
Fletcher Margaret D
Fletcher Peggy E
Fletcher Peter R
Fletcher William
Flitton Raymond S
Fossey Daphne
Fossey Keith
Fossitt Betty L J
Fowler Annie E
Fowler Barbara E E
Fowler Doris
Fowler Gladys M
Fowler James
Fowler Janet
Fowler John H
Fowler Kathleen
Fowler Margaret L
Fowler Melvyn
Fowler Peter J
Fowler Philip J
Fowler Shirley
Fowler William S
Fowler Winifred May
Fox Arthur
Fox Joan
Fox Richard S
Fox Roger M
Fox Stanley
Frazer Stuart
Freeman John
Friend Linda
Friend Patrick J
Froggatt Rita E
Fuller Anthony
Fuller Dennis G
Fuller Douglas G
Fuller John
Fuller Maureen
Fuller Ronald
Fuller Sandra
Fuller Terence J
Gadsden Mary
Gadsden Thomas
Gale Michael
Gale Rita
Galloway Lynda M
Galloway Rodney
Galloway Terence F
Gambrill Robert S
Gammage Joyce
Garner Elsie M
Garner Reginald
Garner Robert
Garrity Michael J D
Gasson Florrie
Gasson Oliver
Gauge Colin
Geeves Peter K
George F Howard
George Iris
George Marjorie
George Michael J
George Molly H
Gibbs Arthur
Gibbs Denis
Gifford Jane E
Gilbert Beryl
Gilbert Hilary D
Gilbert Malcolm T
Gilbert Rosemary
Gilbert Stuart J
Giles Gordon
Gill Raymond C
Gillinge Melanie A
Gladman Denis
Gladman Dennis H
Gladman Janice S
Gladman June
Gladman Kenneth W
Gladman Paul A
Glynn Gordon F
Glynn Joyce
Glynn Roy
Gobby Mildred M
Goble Mandy
Goble Roy F
Goble Trevor
Goddard Margaret D
Goodship Alan B
Goodship Clive
Goodson Peter K
Goodwin Anthony
Goodwin Peter
Goodwin Roland A
Goragon Laila
Gordon Albert
Gordon Alex D
Gordon Betty E
Gordon Catherine A
Gordon Clara
Gordon Gerald
Gordon Jacqueline M
Gordon John
Gordon Mary
Gordon Peter R
Gordon Robert G
Gordon Rosemary
Gordon Vera
Goss Denis
Gough Peter
Goulding Joseph M
Graham Jessie W
Graham June R
Graham Walter A
Gravelle Jane
Gray Aubrey C
Gray Donald
Gray Marjory
Green Clive
Green Janet
Green Susan E
Green Vivien L
Greengrass Eileen
Greenwood Linda J
Greenwood Stephanie I
Greenwood Stephen G
Griffin Karen
Griffiths Derek A
Griffiths William G E
Grimwade David J
Groom Jessie G
Groom Leslie J
Groom William P H
Groucutt David
Groucutt Lee
Guess Winifred F
Gulliver Greta
Gulliver Greta R
Gutteridge Eileen
Hagger Lilian
Hagger Victor W
Hale Maud
Hale William J
Hall Doris E
Hall Gordon F W
Hall Jean
Hall Kenneth J
Hall Mary M
Hall Richard H S
Hall Ronald A H
Hall Sandra E A
Hall Shirley
Hammond June
Hammond Richard L
Hancox Richard
Hancox Rosalie A
Hansford Graham M A
Hanson Johan
Hanson Juri M
Hanson Madli S
Harbottle Geoffrey
Hardiman Russell
Hardy Marjorie H
Hardy Peter
Harris Aubrey
Harris Bernard H A
Harris Beryl J
Harris Bruce
Harris Cynthia M
Harris Dorothy J
Harris Douglas
Harris Jack
Harris Jean
Harris Joanna R
Harris Kathryn L
Harris Margaret
Harris Nellie
Harris Norman D K
Harris Norman W
Harris Paul
Harris Raymond
Harris Robert
Harris Robert G
Harris Ronald
Harris Royston
Harris Stanley
Harris Stephen R
Harris Winifred
Harrison George L
Harrison Margaret J
Harrison Mary E
Hart Bertie
Hart David A G
Hart Richard G F
Hawes Clive K
Hawes David
Hawes Thomas H
Haycock William
Hayes Angela

Hayes Michael
Haynes Mavis W
Haynes Reginald
Haynes William H
Heady Susan
Heatley Lilian H
Heeps Gordon
Heeps Linda M
Hercock Florence
Hercock Francis G
Hercock James A
Hercock Violet A
Herring Bruce B
Herring Francis W
Herring Keith A
Hewgill Daisy I
Hicks Olive M
Higho Cyril J
Higho Joan
Higho Norman W
Higho Peter
Hill Sandra L
Hillard Kevin E
Hillard Robert
Hillyard Gwen B
Hillyard Valerie G
Hilyard Ronald
Hine Joan
Hinks Francis H
Hinks Harold T
Hinks Sheila C
Hiscock Linda
Hoar Robert
Hoar Susan C
Hobbs Basil D
Hobbs Daphne E
Hobbs Gerald D
Hobbs Janice
Hobbs Jean E
Hobbs John C
Hobbs John R
Hobbs Lesley
Hobbs Margaret A
Hobbs Margaret B
Hobbs Patricia
Hobbs Paul V
Hobbs Raymond
Hobbs Richard B
Hobbs Susan
Hodgson Derek
Holliday Emily L
Hollingsworth Ann
Holman Geoffrey C
Holman Kathleen M
Holman Michael F
Holman Sidney F
Holman Valerie A
Holmes Anthony
Holmes Edna L
Holmes Patricia A
Holvey Roger A
Hopewell Clifford
Hopewell John
Horning Linda R
Horning Vivienne M
Horton Betty
House Doris
House Joan
Howard George E
Howell Annie
Howlett Maureen
Howlett Patricia M
Howlett Veronica
Hucklebridge Madge
Hucklesby Alan J
Hucklesby Alfred
Hucklesby Bertie
Hucklesby David
Hucklesby George
Hucklesby Georgette
Hucklesby Irene G
Hucklesby Madge
Hucklesby Maisie J
Hucklesby Olive
Hucklesby Rose
Hucklesby Sidney
Hucklesby Sidney A
Hucklesby Susan M
Hucklesby Vera
Hucklesby William M
Hull Jack
Hulse Brian E
Hulse Joyce L
Humphrey Leon W G
Humphreys David H
Humphreys Philip M
Hunter Marjorie
Hyde Bernard
Hyde Betty L
Hyde Denis W
Hyde Dorothy
Hyde Eileen
Hyde Lesley E
Hyde Paul D
Hyde Susan F
Hymus Cyril
Hymus Dora E T
Hymus James
Hymus John
Hymus Kenneth
Hymus Leslie F
Hymus Lilian
Hymus Norman
Hymus Roy G
Hymus Sicilia M
Hymus Trevor H
Impett Betty O
Impey Donald
Innell Ivy or Joy
Innell Zero
Ireland Fred
Ireland Mary
Ireland Mavis
Ireland Priscilla L
Irons Kathleen
Irving Laura
Itzinger Derek
Itzinger Jennifer
Itzinger Kenneth C
Itzinger Linda E C
Itzinger Mary E
Itzinger Ronald
Itzinger Susan
Jackson David
Jackson Eileen
Jackson Pauline
Jackson Sylvia
James Alec G
James David J
James Edward L
James Elizabeth Glenys
James James A
James Kenneth
James Linda Ann
James Margaret K
James Michael
James Robert
Jamieson Patricia
Jamieson Robert D
Janes Frank E
Janes Kenneth J
Janes Mary E
Janes Peter J
Janes Ronald L
Janes Stella M
Jarvis David R
Jarvis John
Jarvis John R
Jeeves Alan J
Jeeves Doreen
Jeeves Jacqueline
Jeeves Jillian
Jeeves Shirley
Jeffiries Kathleen
Jeffries Anthony J
Jeffries Michael
Jeffries Peter J
Jeffs Richard J
Jellis Aubrey F
Jellis Betty
Jellis Florence M
Jellis Fred
Jellis Louie
Jellis Peter F
Jellis Sheila A
Jellis Violet
Jerone Jon P
Jessop Janice
Jessop Susan
Jobson John
Jobson Joy
Johnson Arthur
Johnson Arthur J
Johnson Lila V
Johnson Ruby R
Johnson Sheila D
Jones Alan E
Jones Barry
Jones Brenda :L
Jones Brett
Jones Brian A
Jones Christina
Jones Gwendoline A
Jones Margaret A
Jones Roger
Jones Ruby A
Jones Trevor G
Jubb Geoffrey
Jubb Helen B
Jubb Philip A
Katz Robin B
Keeble Keith
Keeble Roy
Keeble Yvonne A
Kemp Fraser C
Kemp Jane
Kemp Susan C
Kempton Derek J
Kempton Jillian
Kempton John
Kempton June A
Kempton Margery
Kennard Ian W
Kennard Iris B
Kennard Raymond
Kennard Rita E
Kennard Warden F
Kent Aileen E
Kent Barbara J
Kent Yvonne
King Lesley
King Mary J
King Stephen
Kingham Arthur
Kingham Doris
Kingham Edith
Kingham Gladys
Kingham Margaret A
Kingham Michael L
Kingham Paul
Kingham Peter
Kingham Una
Kings Susan M
Kiser Sheelagh L
Kitchiner Brian R
Kitchiner Jacqueline M
Kitchiner John
Kitchiner Rona P
Kitchinman Barry
Kitchinman Peter
Klimes Anthony
Knight Arthur
Knight Beatrice
Knight Florence

Knight Irene
Knight Robert
Knight Ronald
Knight Ronald G
Knight Sheila M
Knight Stella M
Konefski Grace
Konkiel D M
Konkiel Pauline A
Kunert Rosemary A
Kutock Beth
Kutock Martin
Lacham Herbert T
Laidlaw Alexander
Laidlaw Duncan
Laidlaw Fraser
Laing Barry N
Laing Joy N
Lamb Brenda
Lamb Jennifer D
Lambert Trevor C
Lampert Helen
Lane Chrstine
Lane Cyril
Lane Edna
Lane Edward L
Lane Eva
Lane Leslie George
Lane Linda C
Lane Patricia
Lane Terence A
Lang-Sadler Elizabeth
Lapthorne Carole
Larby Michael J
Larman Bertram F
Larman Maisie B J
Lattimer Bryan
Lawman Derek
Lawrence Rose
Leach Florrie
Leach Herbert
Ledster Marie
Lee Barbara
Lee Barry J
Lee Hazel
Lee Joan
Lee John A
Lee Joyce
Lee Keith
Lee Neville Stuart
Lee Patrick
Legg Eric
Leggett Jacynth A
Lemon Sheila
Leonard Muriel E
Lewis Sidney O
Lewsey Derek
Lewzey Kathleen
Lewsey Sylvia
Lewzey Valerie
Lilley Jean D P
Lilley Pamela M P
Little Barbara A
Little C John
Little Margaret J
Little Sheila M
Loader Janice A
Locking Peter
Loveridge Elizabeth M
Loveridge Kisby
Loveridge Violet
Loveridge Violet
Lowe Malcolm F
Lowin William
Lucas Frederick
Lunn Pamela
Lunn Pamela R
Luty Mavis
Lynch Christopher
MacAlpine Margaret
MacDonald Lawrence
Mack Ronald
Mackenzie Christopher
Mackenzie Helen
Mackin Paul F J
Maher Barbara
Maily Heather
Maily Liam
Major Gillian M
Major Michael
Major Roger G
Major Trevor
Mallard Robert
Mallett George
Mann John
Manning Gregory
Manning Jan
Marlow Christopher
Marlow Elaine S
Marlow George
Marlow Jennifer L
Marlow Robert
Marlow Susan
Marriott Colin J
Marshallsey Nicholas
Martin Caroline
Martin John
Martin Leonie M
Martin Margaret
Martin Stephen G
Mathi Yvonne
Maughan Colin
Maule Jean
Mauser Margaret
Mayhew Angela M
Mayhew Peter R
Mayhew Roger C
Mayhew William H
McAlphine Kathleen
McAlpine Pauline
McEleny Margaret
McEleny Rena
McGowan Margaret B
McGowan Paul
McGowan Peter J J
McLellan Alexander J
McLaughlin Christine
McLaughlin Patrick
McLaughlin Sharon
McLellan Isobel J
McLellan Margaret
McLellan Marian
McMillen Alan
McMillen Barry
Meadows Adrienne
Meadows Betty
Meadows Enid M
Medhurst Reginald
Meeks Audrey E
Megson Carol B
Mepham Andrew
Meynell Pat
Milburn Annie N
Millard David J
Millard Susan J
Miller Helen
Miller Jean
Miller Stanley J
Mills John
Milton Edward
Milton Jeremy
Mockridge June H
Moloney Mark
Molyneaux Catherine A
Molyneaux David V
Molyneaux John
Moore Gillian P
Moore Pamela J
Moore Shirley C
Moran Roger
Moreton Jean
Morgan Ann
Morgan Vivienne M
Moriarty Sheila
Morris Roy
Morrison Ewan
Morrison Jean
Mort Marilyn B
Moulton Elsie
Moulton Ena
Moulton Leslie
Mountfort Kathleen A
Mountfort Mary E
Mountfort Stephen R
Mountfort Victor C
Muckleston Angela
Muckleston Anthony
Muckleston Beatrice M
Muckleston Betty M
Muckleston Cynthia
Muckleston Daphne P
Muckleston Derek
Muckleston Edith
Muckleston Eileen M
Muckleston Elsie
Muckleston Ethel
Muckleston Ida
Muckleston Ivy
Muckleston Jack
Muckleston Joyce
Muckleston Les H
Muckleston Patricia D
Muckleston Percy
Muckleston Peter R
Muckleston Ronald
Muckleston Rupert E
Muckleston Sheila M P
Muckleston Tom
Muckleston Verna W
Muckleston W
Munnett Roger
Murch Julian
Murray Gerald T
Murrray Stewart
Muskett Ivy W
Muskett Jack
Muskett Stanley W
Nash Colin E D
Nash Edna
Neal Ronald
Neal Keith
Neal Lily
Neal Mabel
Neal Ronald
Neale Anne
Nelson Donald R
Newitt David J
Newitt Maureen A
Newitt Raymond C
Newton Peter
Newton Royston J
Nicholls Anne E
Nicholls David
Nicholls David G
Nicholls Norah M
Nicholls Roger
Nicholls Susan A
Niener Terence
Nightingale Susan D
Norris Alan
Norris Pamela
Norris Tony
Northern Philip W C
Northern Susan V A
Norton Colin
Nunn Graham
Nye Martin
Oakley Jean
Oakley Joan
Oakley Marion
Oakley Pauline
Oakley Thelma M
Oakley Veronica B
Oakley William

Odell Barry
Odell Daphine B
Odell Dorothy
Odell Howard L
Odell Sheila
Oliver Diane
Oliver John E
Oliver Judith A
Oliver Pamela J
Oliver Robert G
O'Neill Edward A
O'Neill Jean
O'Neill Norman L
O'Neill Raymond
Oribine Margaret
Ormerod James A
Osborn Christine Y
Osborn Kenneth W
Osborne Colin P
Osborne Doreen
Osborne Richard W
Page Antony B
Page Clifford
Page Frederick
Page James A
Page John
Palmer Angela K
Palmer Anthony M
Palmer Diane B
Palmer Gloria R
Palmer Pauline M
Palmer Ronald
Parker Albert
Parker Daisy
Parker Diane
Parker Eliza
Parker Garry E
Parker June E
Parker Kay F
Parker Montague
Parker Patricia
Parker Philip E
Parker Rene
Parker Uriah
Parrack Mildred
Parrack Muriel
Parrot Douglas
Parrott Elsie
Parrott Gillian C
Parrott Jennifer
Pateman Carole
Pateman Clifford L
Pateman Corrine
Pateman Doreen
Pateman Jean M
Pateman Leslie
Pateman Mary E
Pateman Richard
Pateman Stephen E
Pateman Valerie K
Pateman William
Pateman Willian J
Paterson Daniel
Paterson Nancy
Paterson Patricia A
Paterson Robert G
Pates Arthur G
Patrick Enid
Patrick Vera G
Patterson David
Patterson Fred G
Patterson Jane S J
Patterson Susan
Patteson Gordon
Pattison Sylvia
Paxton Gillian A
Pay Cecilia A
Pay David J
Pay Elizabeth M
Pay Margaret A
Payne David R
Payne Derrick G
Payne Gerald
Payne Leslie J
Payne Margaret A
Payne Sheila L
Peach Bernard J
Peach Francis
Peach Gerald F
Peach Ian J
Peach Leopold J W
Peach Lilian M
Peach Mabel L
Peach Oswald D
Peach Peter
Peachey Richard
Pearman Grace
Pears David M
Pears Heather
Pears Janet
Pears Margaret
Peasland David G
Peasland Michael
Peck Albert C
Peck Hilda A
Peck Iris W
Peck James D T
Peck June P
Peck Marion A
Peck Nelson
Peddar Alex
Peddar Catherine
Peddar Christopher
Peddar Eric
Peddar Freda
Peddar Geoffrey V J
Peddar Janice
Peddar Myra
Peddar Philip R
Peddar Victor J W
Perrin Andrew M
Perrin Margaret E
Perry Davia
Perryman Mary
Peters Jonathan H
Petryszyn Kenneth J
Petryszyn Michael G
Petryszyn Stephen P
Pett Ivor
Pett John G
Pett Kathleen E
Pett Nigel A
Pett Rita M
Pett Valerie H
Phillips Jesse M
Philpott Winifred
Phipps Derek
Pierce Susan G
Piper Raymond W
Plaine Basil F
Pollard Jean
Pollard John W
Pollard Kenneth H
Pollard Pauline
Pollard Sheila
Pope Michael
Porter John M
Porzic Anne-Maria
Pottle Christina
Potts Kathleen
Powell (Aldersey) Roy
Powell Dorothy M
Powell Gwennie I
Powell Jennifer
Powell Jennifer E
Prince Audrey
Prince Colin
Prince Edward
Prince Marion J
Prince Pamela J
Prince Philip
Prince Ronald
Prince Vera
Prince William
Prince William
Proctor Jean
Proctor Raymond
Pugh George
Pugh Jean
Purser Adrian E
Radall Barbara
Ramsden Paul L
Ramsden Susan J
Randall Austin
Randall Bertie
Randall Doreen F
Randall Frances
Randall Horace
Randall Joan
Randall Joyce P
Randall Kenneth
Randall Marjorie
Randall Mary
Randall Olive
Randall Roma S
Randall Susan C
Randall Wilfred
Randell Bryan Austin
Ray Ethel
Raymond Goodwin
Rayson Judith W
Rees Nigel
Reeves Adrian N
Reeves Eileen
Reeves Jacqueline A
Reeves Kathryn J
Reeves Lawrence S W
Renwick Richard R
Renwick William F L
Reynolds Rosalind A
Rhodes John W
Richardson Alan
Richardson David J
Richardson Mary J
Ricks Ian M P
Riding John
Roberts Bryan S
Roberts George A
Roberts Jean
Roberts Nellie
Roberts Peter
Roberts Richard
Roberts Rosemary
Roberts Stephen
Robins Gaynor A
Robinson Christopher J
Robinson Daphne A
Robinson Diane
Robinson Evelyn
Robinson Norah
Robinson Patricia E E
Robinson Richard
Robinson Vera N
Roe Sally
Rogers Elizabeth T
Rogers Gertrude M L
Rogers Jack
Rogers James T
Rogers Kathleen
Rogers Lily
Rogers Margaret
Rogers Margaret
Rogers Mary A T
Rogers Norman
Rogers Peggy
Rogers William C
Roos Florence
Roos Sheila
Roos Victor
Rowe Anne
Rowe Geoffrey B
Rowe Margaret E
Rowe Maurice J
Rowe Paul V

Rowe Peter
Rowe Susan C A
Rowles Barry
Rowles Julie D
Rowles Philip R
Rowley Eileen R
Ruhl Oliver V
Russell Alan
Russell Aubrey
Russell Ian
Russell Morton F
Russell Sheila
Ryan John
Samm Allan A
Samm Gwyneth G
Samm Lauri L
Sanders June M
Sandifer John R
Saunders Davina
Saunders Donald R
Saunders Edith
Saunders Edward
Saunders Florence L M
Saunders George
Saunders Georgina
Saunders Gwendoline R
Saunders Kenneth
Saunders Mervyn
Saunders Sylvia A
Saunders William
Saunders Winifred
Scott Rita K
Scrivener Josephine
Scrivener Nora
Sears Peter
Seaward Denise L
Seaward Lorraine O
Seebohn Alison P
Seed Doris M A
Selfe Patricia
Sells Douglas W
Sells Grace C
Sells Gwyneth L
Sells Joseph H
Sells Millicent R
Sendall Jacqueline A
Sewyer John
Seymour Rosanna M
Sharp Margaret
Sharp Pauline
Shaw Diana V
Sheehan Marlyn K
Sheehan Patrick V
Shelton Denis G
Shelton Geoffrey H
Shelton John
Shelton Richard H
Shepherd Christopher
Shepherd Margaret E
Shepherd Melvin
Shepherd Michael
Shepherd Sandra
Shepherd Thelma
Shepherd Thomas H
Shepherd Thos
Shepherd Wendy A
Shepherd William
Sheppard Ivor J
Sheppard Jean M
Sheppard Lesley J
Sherratt Peter T
Shipp Brian A
Shipp Denis G
Shipp Margaret
Shipp Rosemary
Sickler Roy
Sickler Stanley R
Sillence Derek
Sillense David
Silver Carissa D
Silver Melvin J
Silverstein Hyman
Silverstein Marie
Simmonds Alice
Simmonds Ann
Simmonds Christine
Simmonds Eileen M
Simmonds Howard A
Simmonds Ian J
Simons James J H
Simpkin Gillian
Simpson Gail S
Sinfield Gary
Sinfield Raymond D
Single Andrew G
Single Chris A
Single Ian G
Skeer Eileen F
Skeer Janice
Smart Barbara I
Smart Martin W
Smith Winifred
Smith Alan G
Smith Alan M
Smith Albert J
Smith Ann P
Smith Anthony
Smith Archibald C
Smith Betty M
Smith Christine A
Smith Christine Anne
Smith Cissie
Smith Clifford L
Smith Daphne I
Smith David
Smith David G
Smith Doreen E
Smith Douglas
Smith Elizabeth
Smith Elsie
Smith Eva C
Smith Frances
Smith Frank
Smith Freda J
Smith Frederick G
Smith Gwendoline
Smith Hubert
Smith Ian G
Smith Irene E
Smith Isabella
Smith James A
Smith Jean A
Smith John
Smith John Philip
Smith Joseph S
Smith Kathleen M
Smith Keith
Smith Leonard G
Smith Louie
Smith Margaret E
Smith Margaret L
Smith Marjorie
Smith Mary
Smith Mavis
Smith May
Smith Michael C
Smith Nancy
Smith Nathan
Smith Norman H
Smith Patricia J
Smith Peter
Smith Peter F
Smith Peter J
Smith Philip J
Smith Phyllis R
Smith Queenie
Smith Raymond
Smith Reg F
Smith Reginald E
Smith Robert G
Smith Robert J
Smith Rodney
Smith Ronald G
Smith Shirley
Smith Shirley A
Smith Sidney
Smith Stanley
Smith Stewart
Smith Suzanne W
Smith Sylvia
Smith Terence V
Smith Tom F
Smith Violet
Smith Violet R
Smith Vivien M
Smith William A
Smith Winnie
Sneddon Audrey
Sneddon Richard
Snoxall Susan
Soames David
Soames Douglas
Solly Bernard
Soper Malcolm
Sowden Geoffrey L
Sowden Jack L
Spanswick Alan J
Sparkes David
Sparkes Elsie
Speyer Susan
Spragg Barbara
Squires Lesley C
Stanley John R
Stanford David T
Stanford Mary E
Stanghon Christopher
Stanghon Cissie
Stanghon Philip
Stanghon Richard J
Stanley Janet
Stanley Mary L
Stanley Reginald G W H
Stanton Clifford D
Stanton Marjorie J
Stanton Raymond A
Stanton Thelma M
Stapleton Carol A
Stapleton Christina M
Stapleton Reginald
Stapleton Violet E
Stein Bernard
Stevenson Douglas G
Stewart Carol
Stewart David
Stewart G W
Stewart Ian
Stewart Ian A
Stewart Jean
Stimson Charles
Stone Alan
Stone Brian A
Stone Carol
Stone Donald C
Stone Grace
Stone Robert W
Stone Trevor
Stone Vera D I
Stoneman June R
Storrar Helen
Storrar Ronald H
Stotesbury June D
Stringer Arthur
Stringer Doris
Stringer Fred
Stringer Lyn S
Stringer Malcolm R
Stringer Reginald
Stringer Stuart J
Stringer Victor
Stripp Brian R
Strudwick Eliza M
Struggles David M
Struggles Peter
Sturgeon Frances

Sturgeon Ruth
Suker Alan
Summerfield Elsie
Swain Anthony
Swain Mary T
Swain Pauline
Swain Robert
Tabard Jonathan P
Tabard Martin H
Tann John S
Tawell John R H
Taylor Clement B P
Taylor Ellen E
Taylor Henry
Taylor Jacquline A
Taylor Jill
Tew David R
Tew Derry A
Thomas David B
Thomas Michael
Thomas Sarah
Thompson Dolly V
Thompson Mabel
Thompson Shirley
Tiler Sophie
Tiller Bryan
Tiller Jill L
Tiller John Derek
Tilling Andrew J
Tilling Anne
Tilling Glynn
Tilling Raymond E
Timms Marjorie
Timms Patricia A
Timms Seton
Timms Stephen A
Timms Valerie
Tolleth Margaret M
Tomblin Shirley
Tomlins Eric F
Tompkins Mary R
Tompkins Paul G
Tucker Daphne J
Tugwood George
Turner Andre C
Turner Diane S
Turner Roger
Turney Alan C S
Turney Basil S
Turney Brian
Turney Christine E
Turney Edna B
Turney Eric J
Turney Ivy L
Turney Linda E
Turney Nicholas T
Turney Patricia E
Turney Richard
Turney Walter J
Turney Yvonne
Tutt Edward G
Tutt Elaine I
Tutt Patricia A
Uden Constance
Underhill Roslyn M
Underwood Joan
Underwood Winifred L
Upton Kevin J
Van Mindene H
Vause Peter John
Ventham Stanley
Wade William
Wadsworth Sylvia M B
Wainwright Jean M
Wainwright Peter
Wakelin Steven J
Walker Dorothy
Walker Gordon N
Walker Jennifer R
Walker Maria E
Walker Susan M
Walters Edna M
Walters Harry
Walters Iris J M
Walters Michael
Walters Susan M
Walters Thomas
Walton Eva M
Warburton Clive A
Warburton Ian B
Warby David W
Ward Barbara R E
Ward Brenda
Ward Carol A
Ward Catherine E
Ward Colin
Ward David L
Ward Dennis R
Ward Gladys
Ward Glynis
Ward Joan
Ward Madeline
Ward Maureen
Ward Michael
Ward Michael J
Ward Philip R
Ward Raymond
Ward Reg A A
Ward Winifred
Warren Ethel L
Washington Gwendolen
Washington Joseph
Washington Marjory
Waters Chrstine M
Waters David G
Waters Martin
Watts James E
Watts Joyce
Watts Paul
Weatherley Miriam A
Weatherly Ruth H
Webb Dorothy V
Webb Mary D L
Webster Stephanie D
West Peter C
Whalley Michael D
Whipp Marjorie
Whipp Roger
Whitbread Alice G
Whitbread Eileen L
Whitbread Jacqueline
White Bernard W
White Clive
White Conrad
White Helen G E
White James S
White Janet I
White Mabel
Whitman Norma
Wickens Derek
Wickens Patricia M
Wiggett Nicola J
Wild Ada Jessie
Wild Ian G
Wiley Jill M
Wiley Paul M
Wilkins Olive L
Wilkins Ronald
Wilkinson Mary
Williams Barry
Williams Christine L
Williams Elvira
Williams Jacqueline M
Williams Jeffrey M
Williams John A
Williams Kevin C
Williams Mary E
Williams Rosemary M
Williams Wendy R
Williams-Yeagers Valerie
Willis Alfred S
Willis Christopher J
Willis John
Willis Margaret
Willis Rosemary
Willison David J
Willison Joan
Willison Paul
Wilson Douglas
Wilson Jean
Windmill Lesley
Winkworth Peter J
Winkworth Peter J
Withington Diana M R
Witney Selina
Witney William
Wolski Roger S
Wond Alice
Wond Edith Mary
Wond Winifred
Wood Alice
Wood Geo
Woodcock Ann
Woodfield Ronald
Woodham Marion
Woodham Pamela S
Woodhead Edith
Woods David A
Woods George
Woods Margaret
Wooliscroft David J
Wooliscroft James
Wooliscroft Maureen P
Worsfold Paul
Worsfold Peter
Wren John
Wright Daphne C M
Wright Doreen E
Wright Henry V
Wright Nora J L
Wright William
Wright William C
Wrigtht Colin A
Yates Alan
Yates Amy E
Yates Ann
Yates Anthony
Yates Doris E
Yates Ellen M
Yates Eric B
Yates Irene
Yates Jimmy
Yates John
Yates Marjory R
Yates Maurice J
Yates Pauline
Yeagers William V
Yeomans Alan R
Yeomans David
Yeomans Lorna
Young Lily M
Young Susan

Headteachers

Among the headteachers of the schools there have been:

National /Primary School:

Mr W.Rapsey	(? – 1864)
Mr E.Billingham	(1865-1874)
Mr C.E. Thomas	(1875-1914)
Mr B. Wootton	(1914-1950)
Mr R. Dillingham	(1950-1967)

St George's Primary/Lower:

Mr R. Dillingham	(1967-1977)
Mr Lymbery	(1977-?)

Other heads have included Jean Jennings, Helen Cook and Alex Thorpe.

Mrs J. Spencer	(2005-)

Wesleyan School: F.C. Sommerton 1905-1909

Council School:

Mr J.M. Wilson (temporary head 1909/10)

Mr F.C. Sommerton	(1910-1932)
Mr E. Shepherd	(1932-1947)

Secondary Modern School:

Mr F. Young	(1947-1951)
Mr K.A. Pascoe	(1951-1953)
Mr J.W. Fewson	(1953-1963)

Parkfields Secondary/Middle:

Mr J.W. Fewson	(1963-1973)
Mr D Calcott	(1974-2001)
Mr David Brandon-Bravo	(2001-)

In September 1967 the infants school moved from the old 'National' School buildings in Station Road and the juniors from the 'Council' buildings in Leighton Road to the present site in Manor Road. The new school was called St George of England School, a name showing the connection with the Parish Church of the same title. There were now 419 children, aged 5 to 11 on the roll, organised into 10 classes giving an average of 42 children per class.

In the official opening program, dated Wednesday 17 July 1968 , J.C. Barker, County Architect, described the building as follows:

'The building comprises ten classrooms designed in five separate pairs, with two classrooms situated on the first floor. The central assembly hall looks out on to the swimming pool [now long gone] on one side, and an open court and paved teaching area facing south, the building acting as a natural wind barrier during outdoor activity periods.

Messrs J.M. Hill & Sons (Ampthill) Ltd of Ampthill were the general contractors, completing the school some four months ahead of schedule for a contract sum of £87,253 which represented one of the most economical schools erected by this Authority.'

Managers of the School:
Chairman: County Alderman D.W. Hyde, plus The Rev W. Bevis, County Councillor A. Soskin , R. Cawley Esq, W.A. Childs Esq, G.V. Peddar Esq.
Correspondent: M. Wootton Esq.
Members of the Staff:
Headteacher: Mr R. Dillingham, Deputy Head Mr F.R. Lamb, Assistant Staff: Mrs M. Mountfort (Head of Department), Mr J.M. Fern (Graded Post), Miss E.O.W. Troubridge, Mr D. Morgan, Mrs A.H. Morgan, Mrs S. Crossley, Mrs J. Penson, Mrs A. Burrows, Mr W.B. Deeley.
Clerical Assistants: Miss D. Bates, Mrs M.B. Dillingham. Cook Supervisor: Mrs F. Youens.
Caretakers: Mrs A. Shepherd, Mrs H. Saunders. Groundsman: Mr S.J. Elk.

New swimming pool, June 1968. Back row: Paul Livemore, Peter Gadsden, Philip Compton, Martin Northall, Haydn Richards. In the middle: Tony Raggett, Tony Sinfield, Brian Weatherley, Susan Dart, Neal Hewison, Christopher Webster, David Cook, Peter Spinlove, Mark Thorniwell, Peter Highnum. Front row: Angela Tutt. Amanda Brewer, Christine Hart, Vanessa Edwins and Martin Webb. Various fund raising events took place over the years to raise the money for this pool, which has now been filled in.

The cast of a nativity play presented by seven-year-olds in the Junior School, 15 December 1967. The class teacher was Mary Mountfort.

St George of England School 1st Netball Team, 1968. Back row: Christine Hart, Gillian Ware, Mrs Fern (teacher), Agnes Elliott, Karen Baker. Front row: Angela Tutt, Pip Brazier and Debbie Berry.

Staff about 1974.
Back row: Roger Norton, Thea Farrow.
Third row: Isabel Pope, Meg Powell, Maggie Bradbury, Marjorie Miles, Jean Brock, Megan Green, Kay McArthur, Amy Shepherd, Sheila Fern.
Second row: Shirley Hawes, Andrée Morgan, Rick Fern, Richard Dillingham, Mary Mountfort, Pat Herring, Anne Eyles.
Front row: Heather Curry, Jean Bainbridge, Linda Dicken, Dee Curtis.

Staff about 1977.
Back row: Margaret Hart, Beryl Green, Jean Brock, Thea Farrow, Kay McArthur, Meg Green, Anne Eyles, Shirley Hawes, Maggie Bradbury, Meg Powell, André Morgan.
Middle row: Sheila Fern, Mary Mountfort, Rick Fern, Richard Dillingham, Mary Dillingham, Amy Shepherd, Roger Norton.
Front row: Jean Bainbridge, Sue Carter.

May 2007 saw the creation of a new form of transport in the form of a 'walking bus'. A walking bus is a form of transport for schoolchildren who are accompanied by two adults, a 'driver' and 'conductor' who walk to school, in much the same way a bus would drive them to school. Like a traditional bus, walking buses have a fixed route with designated 'bus stops' and 'pick up times' in which they pick up the school children. The scheme cuts traffic congestion, helps the environment and improves safety. Traffic outside the main gates is reduced which makes access safer and easier. It was reported that Janet Hicks, member of the Parent Governor Group, played a crucial role in setting up Toddington St George's walking bus.

The school run is never boring for pupils thanks to lollipop lady Sue Adams née Walker who safely sees children and parents across Leighton Road. Sue who first started on the crossing on 14 January 2009 gives out lollipops to the children at the end of every term and on her birthday. She recalled that other School Crossing Patrol Officers have included: Olive Chapman, Ann Hathaway, another Sue Adams, Sharon Wormsley, Lynn Croucher and Mr Kingham.

Toddington Old Boy, Tony Fuller, February 2012, explains to Saint George's Lower School pupils the ancient custom observed at midday on Shrove Tuesday at Conger Hill. He told them about the legend of putting their heads close to the ground and listening to the old witch frying her pancakes in her kitchen under the ground. The earliest reference to the custom in the school log book is dated 1865, which said it was an old custom then. John Pask rang the church 'pancake bell' for five minutes before twelve to summon the children to the hill.

On Friday 16 March 2012, Year 4 children celebrated the end of their WW2 studies by having their own VE Day party. Community members were invited along to share their own war memories with the nine-year- olds and join them for a cup of tea and sandwiches. Guests were also treated to a singing and dancing display.

Wesleyan School Days

The following account was written in 1946 and appeared in the Methodist Church, *Centenary Souvenir Handbook*:

'In 1854 The Wesleyan School was built to be used as a Sunday School and Day School, and we can be proud of the boys and girls who received their earliest education there. Numbered among the old boys are ministers, successful businessmen, schoolmasters and civil servants.

The Day School was opened by Mr Faulkner, who was followed by Mr Quick, Mr Richardson, Mr Pearce and Mr Sommerton as Headmasters. It was closed in 1910 when a new Council School was built, and the building was thereafter known as the Wesley Hall.

A flourishing Sunday School occupied the building on Sundays and many loyal and true men and women have worked as superintendents and teachers. Mr J. Gibbons was one of the earliest superintendents and amongst other well-known workers who have "occupied the desk" are Messrs. Richardson, Quick, Pearce, A. Neale, G. Ashby, G. Ireland, C. Ireland, J. Page, A, Evans, W. Fleckney, H. Nicholls and the present Superintendent C. Falberg.

Old scholars will remember the Sunday School treats, held in Chapel Close, or Dog Kennels, when we formed a procession headed by a brass band on the route for the field. Today motor coaches take the children and friends for a day at the seaside.

Easter Sunday is the Sunday School Anniversary, and the great day of the year, when the singing of the children, and the special preacher draw large congregations. Generally, the hymns are taught by the choirmaster, but many of us have pleasant memories of the days when we were taught by Mr A. Neale.

Our scholars today are fewer in number than in past days but we still have the devoted and faithful friends who Sunday by Sunday endeavour to spread the gospel among our children.

On the walls inside the chapel there are memorial tablets to:
John Cotching and Jane Cotching, his wife; Susan Briden, JA Pitts and Julia Pitts, his wife; Arthur Neale and his wife Martha Neale.'

The following account is taken from *Toddington Memories* by Victor Seymour of his account at the Council School. He started school at the age of three in 1907.

'When it was time for me to start school, much of the authority previously vested in the Anglican and Wesleyan churches had been taken over by the County Council. Attendance was now compulsory between the ages of five and fourteen years and because of this, religious instruction although taught, was optional. Nevertheless some influence has remained; denominational governors were still elected, and the resident Rector or Minister still paid his visits to the appropriate school. If a parent objected to the Religious Instruction given, that parent's child was removed for the lesson with an emphasis rather over conspicuous; never-the-less my eagerness to avoid any lesson possible caused me to toy with the idea of being an objector, but it was necessary for my parents to object also, and this they had no intention of doing unless of course I could undertake to carry out some other more useful work. As my parents, (at least my Mother), were strict Wesleyan Methodists, my school was pre-selected; at three to five years of age voluntary attendance was accepted, and so at three years of age I went to school, my Mother is no doubt thinking that the staff might as well do a bit more to earn their money.

I do not remember much of this time. I know that I was put into a small room with other children, and that we were given some coloured laces to thread through a mat with a wire tool.

After a year I was allowed to stay away for a time. I cannot remember the reason for this or how it was brought about, but I regarded it with satisfaction. As I neared my fifth year, school again began to loom up, and with this no doubt in my mind my mother, when I had misbehaved myself, packed me off to school as a punishment, thinking to get the best of both worlds. I can remember my howls at this drastic treatment, and my dislike for any school lessons, thereafter stemmed from it.

Both schools were of similar shape and construction, with yellow brick walls, slated roofs, and wooden floors that had become by now quite worn, and with large knots standing out. They were rectangular in shape, with a dividing wall inside, running lengthways. One side of this wall was again divided, making two classrooms, while the larger portion was used as an assembly hall and open classroom for several classes with two or three teachers. One of these teachers told me that if she made a joke to her class at one end of the room the laugh often came from the class at the other end, while hers completely missed the point. There was also one extra classroom at the church school abutting the opposite side of the large room, which was necessary to cope with its large attendance. The desks were of the form type, made of pine now blackened and much carved, each seating six pupils. The pinewood has a tendency to splinter into sharp, needle like splinters, and there were accidents.

The school I went to had a gravel yard at the front, about one hundred feet long by fifty feet wide, known as the big playground, and used by the senior boys. Most of the time they spent chasing a small ball, like a pack of hounds in full cry, and it was as well not to be weak or small, if you are caught in that rush. Another small yard at the back of the school almost defies description as a playground. It seems to me that it could not have been more than 15 feet square, and was used by girls and infants. The girls could not do much more than stand in groups and talk, and even then some never seemed to get out of the small cloak room. A six-foot brick wall divided the yard at the back from a field on the outside. All the other sides were enclosed by buildings; these represented the stores, sheds, and utility offices for the school. One was for coke and coal, some of which usually got spilled in the playground as it was being carried in to the school fires, which were in an open fireplace in each small room, and a large slow combustion stove in the large room with a tin chimney stack climbing up the wall. The ashes from the fires had to be taken out and were put in a heap at the side of the yard for removal, and since this yard was on the north side of the school no sun ever entered it. The infants went out to play earlier than the older ones for their safety. A young girl infant teacher went with them, and they played Nuts in May or Ring a Ring of Roses, the words of the rhyme to the last of these being somewhat ironical, "A-tishoo, A-tishoo, we all fall down"; the conditions made both of these more than likely.

The toilets were of the wooden seat with pail under variety, which were emptied twice a week by men who came in the night. The door had a gap of about six inches at bottom and top, and higher still there was a louvre type of slatted ventilation. This kind of ventilation was used throughout the building, allowing a cutting wind and sometimes snow to blow through and clear the stench from the air; the roof was of loose fitting pantiles which had the same effect.

Infectious diseases reached epidemic proportions almost annually, whooping cough, measles, scarlet fever, diphtheria taking their turn, sometimes collectively, to close the school, sometimes for weeks. When the infection was diagnosed, the victim was taken to an isolation hospital some miles away in the country. Here the parents were allowed to visit once a week, but had to stay outside looking at, and trying to speak to, their child through a closed window. They made the journey by pony cart, bicycle or on foot. The house was fumigated by pasting strips of paper around the doors and windows, and burning sulphur inside. The job was done by men from the Council; they were not always very particular about removing the paper seal, and if the poor family were too distressed to do so, the evidence remained for some time, causing us kids as we roamed the streets to somehow connect it with stories we had heard of the plagues in Egypt. I was lucky enough to escape, but not so members of my family. Occasionally the diseases were fatal, and there is no doubt that their unfortunate effects lasted a lifetime

Round about 1910 a new day school was built by the County Council. The Wesleyans lost some of their control and authority, but the church school in Harlington Road continued to be used for another fifty years, and for some time the old rivalry, albeit slowly fading away, continued. It was only when the County Education Committee selected staff replacements irrespective of their denominational inclinations that it completely vanished. It had lasted for many years, sometimes becoming harsh and aggressive; overflowing into other parts of village life, business and political. Later on, the two schools were incorporated into one, and it became completely dead, and the place was better for it.

Our new school was larger, more airy, lighter, with larger playgrounds and an area of garden and grass lawn but many facilities that are now taken for granted did not then exist. Whereas at the old school there had been no drinking water except from the school-house pump, (with permission), now there was a pump, always with lock and chain. Even this did not give proper spring water, and went dry in summer. Inside the Assembly Hall or corridor there were hand basins at each end with taps. The water was rain water, and supplied from large tanks on the roof. I can remember coming in one day, hot, thirsty, and exhausted after a long chase at a game of stag hunt, and taking a quick drink of the water from one of these taps, but unfortunately I was seen by the headteacher, who called me to him, and in the most severe terms told me of all the germs, reptiles, bacteria, and filth that I had been drinking, and also all the after effects I could expect from it at any time during the rest of my life. I still think that a drink of clear water would have been a better answer.

The system of sanitation had not improved in the village, and the lavatories at the new school had only one difference from the previous ones: the seats when sat on caused a cascade of sifted soil to fall from the containing box at the back into the pail. It proved an unsatisfactory arrangement.

After the change-over I was no longer an infant, but became a member of Standard One. The teacher was Miss Edith Dimmock. There were six standards that we could get through in seven years. This meant that at some stage of the way one had to remain in one standard for two years, usually Standard Two or Three. It was best if you could get to six before you stuck, as there was a little more freedom and consideration, and some of the work even began to get interesting. I was lucky enough to get to six.

At Standard One certain changes began to take place and characters began to form. You did not regard anybody that sat next to you with the same indifferent feeling, but had preferences: those that you could trust with a secret and those that you couldn't, and it was more convenient to become friendly with some than others. You were one of a group that you would come to know a lot about in the next seven years, who were going your way, being taught what you were taught, finding out what you found out. Older people would try to lay down guide lines for you to follow, whom to associate with, whom to avoid, small actions would create opinions that would last for ever, and a unique relationship with a group of your own age would be formed that would last a lifetime.

The first three standards were taught by women, with whom you would find more favour if your hair was tidy, your face and shoes clean, and your clothes neat, but at Standard Four came another change, in fact two; we had a master, and there was war. Standards Four, Five and Six were taught by the headmaster, in the same room at the same time. Most subjects had to be taught and marked at different levels, except perhaps, singing and scripture. Looking back now, it is obvious his job was not an easy one. Standard Four, at one side of the room, were still very much juniors in thought and action, while Standard Six at the other side were developing personalities of their own. The teacher needed tact and understanding, and an outside life that had a few other complications. That ours had all three is doubtful, but he had a measure of success

Although in the same room, the Fourth and Sixth standards made little attempt to mix, except perhaps at play time if the Sixth were short of a goalkeeper for the football team, or a fielder at cricket, or if you had a cleaner piece of blotting paper than they had, or an uncrossed pen nib. The sixth form girls were a thing apart, they had nothing to do with the fourth at all, and it was best to keep out of their way if you didn't want to get snubbed to extinction. Sometimes they were used in a superior capacity, as for instance, the making of ink. Ink was made by mixing a blue powder with about half a pail of water; for obvious reasons this was done outside in the playground, and strict supervision was necessary. A couple of us from Standard Four, who of course, saw to it that we could be best spared, were sent out to do this job under the eye of a senior girl - to have sent a senior boy, plus the ink, would have been fatal. The ink when made was put into an enamel jug, taken into school, and poured through a funnel into the ink wells. I can readily picture those two boys walking across the playground carrying the jug and funnel, with inky hands, ink smudged faces and tousled hair, and the girl monitor at a little distance, walking with dignified importance and an air of distaste for her company.

I think singing was the most successful subject. The school was fortunate to have in Standard Six at that time a number of girls who were not only good looking but also had good voices. As the master was an enthusiast for vocal music, the result was an exceptionally fine school choir. This was soon made known to any governors, members of the education committee, or in fact anybody else who visited the school, and should they show more than a passing interest, it was surprising how quickly they found themselves seated in chairs with the choir lined up before them, listening to the tuneful blending of those young voices, which in more cases than not was what they had come to hear. The school inspector was often regarded as an ogre by both staff and pupils, but the one that visited us, Mr Burley, had an Achilles heel - he was musical. Very soon after his arrival the older classes were lined up in the Hall. Miss Maude Hobbs at the piano, was surrounded by the group of pupils with deeper voices, while the sopranos, the Addie girls, and the rest, all joined together in *By Babylon's Waters* and *Oh, Lovely Peace*. Mr Burley usually left quite pleased, and often we were let out early as a reward for our efforts.

When the time came at the end of July 1914, for us to break up for the summer holidays we were all assembled in the main Hall for the head to make his usual speech. Several scholars were leaving, the singing had been of a patriotic nature, and there was a sense of drama. He finished by saying that the present circumstances were like a match being held to a barrel of gunpowder, the explosion was almost certain, before we returned to school there would be war.

When we returned there was indeed war. This was still the age of the Empire, and nearly every subject that we were taught stressed patriotism as a virtue. We knew of men who had fought the Boers, we had heard from our parents of the wild times when Mafeking had been relieved, how they carried beer in buckets up to the ringers in the church tower to keep them going for hours, how they burnt an effigy of Kruger on a huge bonfire on The Green, and how the dancing and revelry went on until the morning hours. We learned how a few years earlier the Campbells had relieved Lucknow, and a girl had been called mad because she said she heard the skirl of their pipes in the distance. We learned and recited with vigour *The Charge of the Light Brigade* and *The Revenge*, and even rehearsed the Battle of Hastings with home-made bows and arrows. This turned out a little unfortunate for me, when a visiting relative, removing her glove to shake hands with one of my parents, found it suddenly pierced by an arrow dropping from the sky.

We were too young to realize the implications of what was taking place around us. The great social and economic change, that was looming up was as yet unseen, and the shock of tragedy for many would be sinking in over the future years. The first noticeable event at school was a visit by some of those boys who had been so recently chasing a ball in the old school playground. They were in khaki now, with leather belts, shining boots, and red shining faces. They always had a bright welcome from our master, which sometimes seemed to surprise them, as some of their antics had not always been as welcome. They were brought into the classroom, still with something that looked like a culprit's grin on their face. Conversations were usually one sided.
"When are you going back?"
"Monday, Sir."
"Did you get our parcel?"
"Yes Sir."
"Have you met any of the other boys?"
"No, Sir, I just missed Harry X, he came up into line the day after I got my leave."
"Would you like me to say anything to the boys in the class?"
"Not much, thanks Sir, only not to be in too much of a hurry."
"Well, thanks for looking in, come and see us again on your next leave and the best of luck."

We heard the polished boots echoing down the corridor, and then the entrance door as it slammed behind them.

It was, of course, necessary to have a flag and a pole. We subscribed and obtained them, painting the pole ourselves as it lay stretched across the playground on two trestles. The sewing class made the flag with the material that was brought, being very careful as they laid the pieces on the floor to set the white part of the white band in its proper order. When it was done it had to be furled correctly so that, when hoisted, a quick flick of the rope would set it free. This had to be practised or the result would be just a bundle at the top of the pole.

Came the time when the German Battle Cruiser Emden was sunk, and we all assembled in the playground, sang *Rule Britannia*, gave three cheers, saluted the flag, and were given a half-day's holiday.

Then there were more solemn times, when there was no talking, and only a little fidgeting. We sang a hymn, then formed around the flagpole in silence as a name was called out, and the flag at half-mast hung limply down. In the road just by, the baker checked his pony, the grocer boy on his bicycle forgot his whistle and the woman with her bag, stopped to look, identified herself with the silence, then went on, muttering to herself, "Poor lad".

At school we were very busy with the war effort, growing more vegetables on the gardens, supporting many causes. For some weeks when blackberries were ripe, we were allowed half days from school to pick them. Vast amounts were gathered to make jam for soldiers, for which we were paid, I think, about a farthing a pound. Boys who wanted to do agricultural work were now allowed to leave at twelve years of age, and many did. In my last year there were two boys and six girls left in the sixth standard, and on my fourteenth birthday my school days came to an end.'

Headteacher Mr Sommerton and dog with lady teachers outside the school entrance. The date 1910 can be seen above the initials on the entrance brickwork. Miss O'Dell can be seen back right.

Early 1900s view of the Wesleyan Methodist School and schoolhouse (right). The school consisted of two classrooms and an assembly hall. The school was built to accommodate 170 pupils. Voluntary attendance before the age of five was encouraged and some pupils started before they were three. Built in 1854, the school closed in 1910 when a new council school was built on adjacent land in Leighton Road. This new building, pictured in 1929, can be seen below. The old assembly hall then became known as the Wesleyan Hall. However some classes were held in the old building in the early 1960s in order to cope with the increase in pupils.

Wesleyan Sunday School Anniversary – The anniversary of this school was celebrated on Easter Sunday, when Mr S.D. Waddy, barrister, of London, delivered two discourses. He also addressed the children in the afternoon in the chapel. The collection amounted to £10. The school now numbers nearly 350 scholars and about 50 teachers. On the Monday following a tea meeting was held in the schoolroom, after which addresses were delivered.

Luton News, 25 April 1865.

Recreation Evenings – The head master, Mr R. Pearce, of the Wesleyan school is taking a new departure this year. On Tuesday he commenced evening class for young men which is to be held three evenings a week at the small fee of one penny. There is to be an hour's instruction and the rest of the time to be taken up with reading and games, daily papers being provided and about 400 books, periodicals and magazines. Prizes will be given at the close of the session to those who have attended, regularly and passed the examination in March.

Luton News, 6 October 1892.

Council School Class , October 1915. Class Standards, covering the different school years, were set mainly for ***R****eading, w****R****iting and a****R****ithmetic. By Standard IV most children would have been able to read a short paragraph from one of the more advanced school reading books, write a sentence dictated slowly and would have been able to work out a money sum. The school leaving age was 12. In 1918 it was raised to 14.*

Headteacher Mr Sommerton and wife with children Donald, Jack and Russell. In 1910 the Beds Education Committee increased the salary of Mr Sommerton from £117 to £120 per annum. On Empire Day (24 May) flags and Union Jacks used to be hoisted on the principle buildings. The schools played their part in the celebrations. Mr Sommerton 'gave an address on Empire' to the children. 'After patriotic drill, The National Anthem, *and three cheers for the King, they were dismissed and half-holidays were given at both schools.'*

Gardening class about 1919. Among those pictured on the back row are G. Baker, C. Hawes and E. Garner. Those pupils on the front row include: F. Muckleston, D. Coles, B. Williamson, K. Hawes and S. Roberts.

Council School, Second Class 1927. Back row: - , Dave Clark, - , Harold Evans, Albert Russell, Dick Collins, Horace Lane, Reg Brazier, Percy Billington, Bill Buckingham.
Midddle row: Arthur Hucklesby, Leslie Garner, Steven Warwick, Douglas Fletcher, Jack Skingsley, Dennis Muckleston, Ivy Hunt, Noran Williams, Hilda Allen, Gladys Coles, Eileen Coles, George Garner.
Front row: Doris Randall, -, Sylvia Mucklestone, Ellen Rowe, Daphne Cleaver, Elsie Kingham, Mary Mucklestone, Doreen Rowe, Cissie Weedon, Gladys Brazier, Eva Kingham, George Holman.

Woodwork class 1930-1 with teacher Eric Fryer standing at back of classroom. Among the back row are: Albert Russell, Victor Kent, Reg Brazier and John Giles.
Front row: Donald Harris, Horace Lane and Harold Evans.

COUNCIL SCHOOL, TODDINGTON.

OPEN SESSION, THURSDAY, 24th. JUNE, 1937.

T I M E - T A B L E.

Class 1. (Mr. E. SHEPHERD.)

1-30 to 2-0.	R e a d i n g.
2-0 to 2-30.	Written English.
2-45 to 3-25.	Art and Cardboard Modelling. (Class 2 Boys.)
3-25 to 3-45.	Singing. (with Classes 2 and 3.)

Class 2. (Miss M. E. KING.)

1-30 to 2-0.	H i s t o r y.
2-0 to 2-30.	Recitation.
2-45 to 3-25.	Needlework and Handwork. (Girls - Classes 1 and 2.)
3-5 to 3-25.	Physical Training. (Girls.)
3-25 to 3-45.	Singing. (with Classes 1 and 3.)

Class 3. (Miss D. RANDALL.)

1-30 to 2-0.	R e a d i n g.
2-0 to 2-30.	H a n d w o r k.
2-45 to 3-5.	Recitation.
3-5 to 3-25.	W r i t i n g.
3-25 to 3-45.	Singing. (with Classes 2 and 1.)

Class 4. (Miss H. M. JEFFS.)

1-30 to 2-0.	E n g l i s h.
2-0 to 2-10.	Dramatisation of Stories.
2-10 to 2-30.	Physical Training.
2-45 to 3-0.	R e c i t a t i o n.
3-0 to 3-35.	H a n d w o r k.

Woodwork Instruction Class 1 Boys, in Manual Training Cen
from 1-30 to 3-45. (Instructor, Mr. E. E. RICKARDS.)

- -

Refreshments at moderate charges, Proceeds for School Funds

Timetable of the Council School, 24 June 1937. The Council School was in competition with the National School for pupils and this open day was an attempt to show what they could do by way of education for their school. There was no National Curriculum in those days and the teachers often taught what they pleased.

School Sports at Toddington in 1941

Toddington Council School met teams from the Church of England School in two events at the Council School Sports. These were relay races for girls and boys, respectively, and each was won by the Council School.

In the other events points were given to the winners of heats and of finals, the child with the highest number being champion in his section. A prize was also given to the winner of each final.

Results:Infants, 50 yards, H. Fulcher; rabbit hop, N. Oakley; glove race, J. Tann; walking race, S. Barham; over and under, N. Oakley; champions, B. Craker and J. Tann (10 points each).

Juniors: 80 yards, G. Arnold; 100 yards, P. Gibbons; three-legged, 8 and 9, L. Anderson and A. Dary; 10 and 11, M. Bevis and J. Soul; high jump, P. Gibbons; long jump, 8 and 9, K. Hunt, 10 and 11, A. Soper; skipping race, 8 and 9, D. Simmonds, 10 and 11, B.Gray; egg and spoon, 8 and 9, K. Hunt, 10 and 11, D. Coleman.

Potato race, 8 and 9, P. Coles, 10 and 11, P. Gibbons; wheelbarrow, 8 and 9, D. Horner and K. Hunt; 10 and 11, L. Hart and B. Oakley; obstacle, 8 and 9, G. Arnold, 10 and 11, R. Anderson; champion, P. Gibbons (19 points).

Seniors: 100 yards boys, J. Arnold and K. Gibbons (dead heat); girls, J. Hobbs; three-legged, girls, J. Hobbs and J. Simmonds; long jump, J. Arnold; obstacle, boys, K. Gibbons; girls, A. Howard; skipping, J. Simmonds; needle-threading, boys, E. Armstrong; throwing the cricket ball, J. Arnold; egg and spoon, mixed, E. Buckingham; potato race, mixed, N. Brinklow; bun-eating, G. Capp.

Relay: girls, J. Hobbs, J. Saunders, J Simmonds and K. Stanghon; boys, J. Arnold, G. Cap, L. Hart and K. Gibbons; champion girl, J. Hobbs (12 points), champion boy, J. Arnold (19 points).

Prizes were distributed in the school on Thursday by Mrs Fawcett, JP, CC. A special prize was handed to L. Brinklow, youngest child in the school, for his gameness and pluck. Community singing brought to a close a very happy and pleasant interlude in the work of the school.

The event was organised by Mr E. Wilmore.

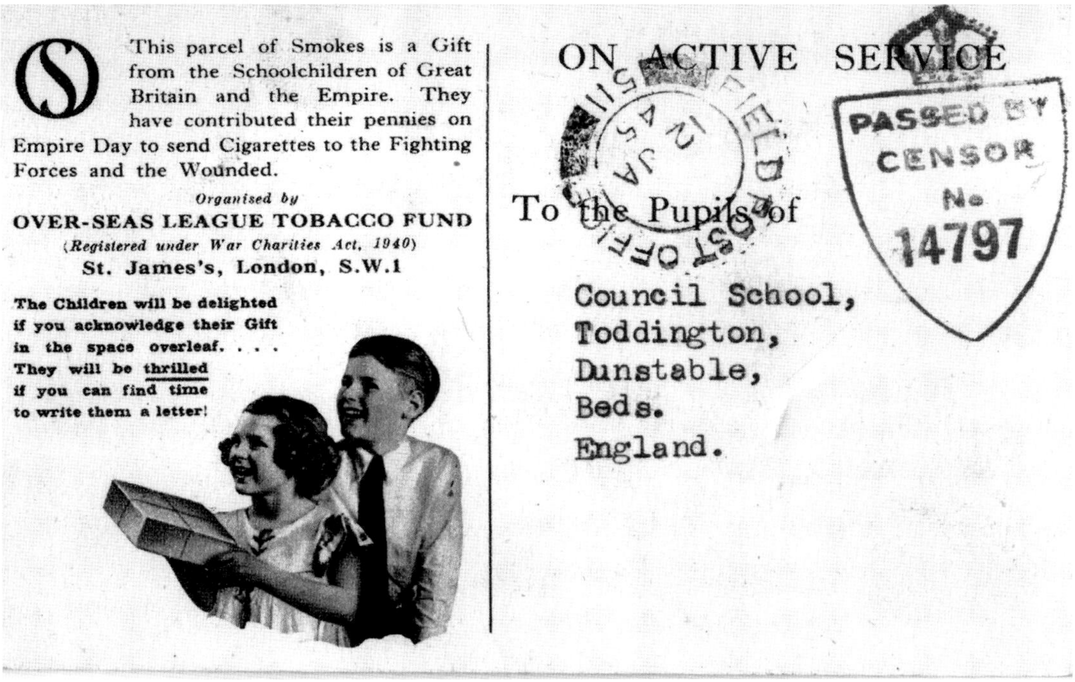

This parcel of Smokes is a Gift from the Schoolchildren of Great Britain and the Empire. They have contributed their pennies on Empire Day to send Cigarettes to the Fighting Forces and the Wounded.
Organised by
OVER-SEAS LEAGUE TOBACCO FUND
(Registered under War Charities Act, 1940)
St. James's, London, S.W.1
The Children will be delighted if you acknowledge their Gift in the space overleaf. . . . They will be thrilled if you can find time to write them a letter!
ON ACTIVE SERVICE
PASSED BY CENSOR No 14797
To the Pupils of
Council School,
Toddington,
Dunstable,
Beds.
England.

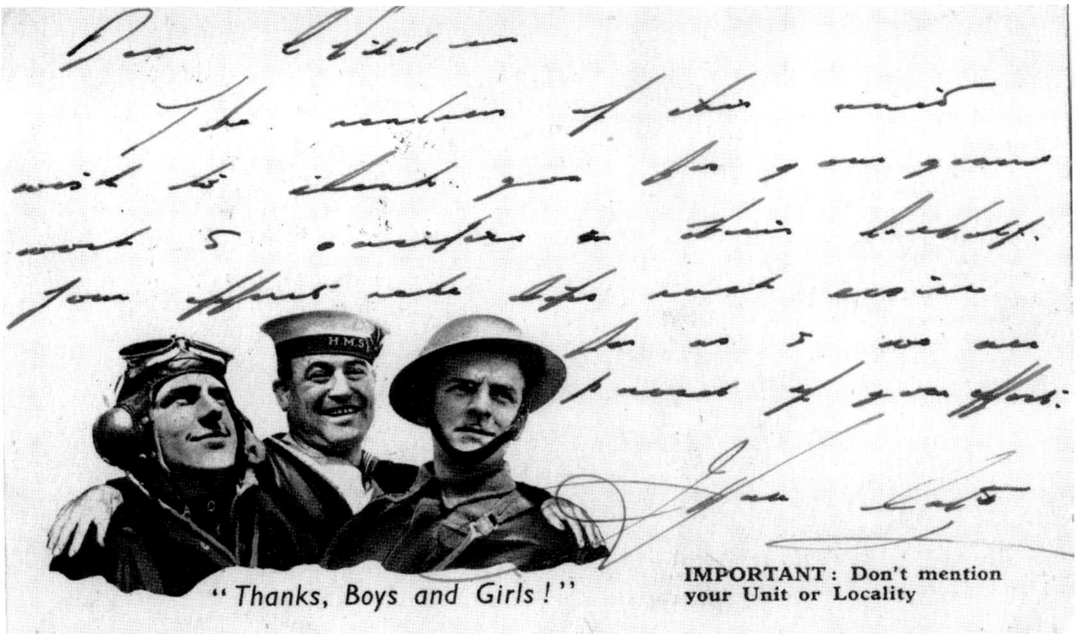

To mark Empire Day cigarettes were sent by the Council School with this card to the men in the 'Fighting Forces and the Wounded'. The card was returned on the 12 August 1945 having been passed by the censor.

Doug Jeeves told the Toddington Old Boys of his wartime schooldays. He had fond memories of Ernest Shepherd reading The Wind in the Willows, *country dancing in the school hall, cricket with Billy Coles; sitting in the school hall during the air raids and singing songs to ease the tension. Although it was wartime he and his friends shared a happy childhood with the community spirit of the time pulling people together.*

Reminiscences

Ron Anderson from London, was evacuated to Toddington in 1940, at the age of 10 with his mother, brother and sister. Ron went to the council school in Leighton Road and enjoyed school dinners. He said: 'They were good dinners and my brother Len and I always looked forward to seconds when available. Mr. Shepherd was the headmaster and we did live, my mum, brother and sister with Mrs Crawley near, I think, the *Griffin* pub near the church.'

Whilst he lived in Toddington Ron spent most of his leisure hours at a farm in Fancott owned by Mr Ireland senior, along with his family, Fred, Priscilla, Mary and of course Mrs Ireland. Fred although older than Ron, was his greatest friend, confidant and teacher, between the ages of 10-15 years when Ron lived in Toddington. Fred was a lovely person to Ron and taught him so many things about the farm and country life that he has never forgotten. 'I cannot remember him ever not answering my constant questions about the farm, countryside or animals, although at times I must have tried his patience.'

'The first time that I went to the farm Fred took me down on the milk float with old Tommy the horse. Fred had his dinner and when he appeared after lunch he was carrying a metal bowl with some funny looking pinchers inside and said that he was going to ring some pigs. He went into the pen and caught the first pig which let out a tremendous squeal; well I thought that he is killing it and ran for all I was worth back to Toddington. When he saw me the next day we really had a good laugh and I was soon an experienced pig ringer's assistant.'

Harold Fletcher left school in 1952, aged 15, to work down that same farm, Feoffee Farm, This is his account of his schooldays:

'I used to love the gardening as I wasn't really one of these clever types. I used to be told to get out of the classroom and stand outside and go and see the headmaster. I tried to do my best. I can remember the teachers: Mrs Joy, Mrs Sadler, Mrs Higgs, Mrs Shaw and Mr and Mrs Wootton. Mr Wootton was the headmaster when I was down the old National School. When we got to about 11 we had to move up from the National School to the Secondary Modern School in Leighton Road – where the village hall is now.

I used to get on well with the headmaster, Mr Fred Young. If we asked for some time off we used to get a blue card, this was given if for example we wanted to go potato picking. Mr Fred Young was alright to us boys. He wouldn't have no nonsense, but we respected him and there was Mr Gilson, Mr Horobin, and Mr Steve Davis. Mr Davis was the PE instructor and if you did anything wrong he would hit you on the backside with his trainer. We used to have PE in the old Wesley Hall which has gone now. We used to do other things, running round the playground for PE and we used to have the football matches up the recreation ground in Luton Road (rec). There were no changing rooms. We used to play in our own shirt. Someone used to have a job keeping the grass cut – it was long grass playing then - no goal posts so we used to put goal posts up. We played other teams like round about such as Northfields and other schools round the area. When we went down to visit the Flitwick school Mrs Shaw always used to lay on bread, butter and jam for a snack – it was great. She was the old timer – but she wouldn't have no nonsense - she was a needlework teacher at the school. There weren't none of this swearing at teachers then – like there is today - you would never do that 'cos your parents would jump down your throat at you and they would punish you for that.

One day I was playing full back and I kicked the ball and knocked Mr Young's trilby off as he was running along the touchline. I thought we would be in trouble but he just said "Play on boys, Play on boys. Play on boys". That was a great time. Then we used to go to Eversholt's swimming pool, on a Seamarks bus but I never could take up swimming – I still cannot swim.

Then another day me and Alfie Dudley played truant. We went down the bottom of the rec one afternoon. There used to be a Walker's bakery where that Kebab shop is now (14 High Street) and we went in there, me and Alfie Dudley and got a currant loaf and walked down the bottom of the rec and stopped down there until about 4 o'clock. My Dad and Bill Dudley, Alfie's dad, were waiting for us when we got home. "Where have you two been? You haven't been down that bloody farm?" My dad laid the law down. He was in the Home Guard – he was a Sergeant Major for a time. We had to stop in the classroom when we went back to school. We had to write down "Do not do that again" write it in the book, you know. That's what we done and we never done it any more, you know.

We always talk about that when we meet – me and Alfie Dudley– you know. All part of school life. We never harmed anybody. And at the school he wasn't in with me with gardening so much as Brian Leary. That's how we won a prize .We used the back garden to grow the vegetables then we used to use the vegetables for the canteen at school. We used to have peas, potatoes, carrots and all the stuff, and used to take it round the kitchen for cooking for the school dinners, no luxury what it is today, used to bring it in a bowl, put so many potatoes - ten of you on a table, then they used to position someone to dish it out at these tables – there used to be a big assembly hall in the secondary modern school, where we used to have our meals.'

Conveniences

The original school toilets were still there in 1951. They were built along the back of the shelter that ran across the play ground. The toilets were not connected to the sewer and consisted of just a bucket with a seat over them. When a pupil sat on the seat a spring was depressed so that when he or she stood up the seat rose slightly causing a sprinkling of sand that was in a container above the toilet to drop into the bucket. The buckets were emptied once a week by the night cart. Unfortunately with the increased number of pupils the buckets would get full before the night cart was due. When this happened, the teacher David Morgan, who taught gardening would ask the class for volunteers to empty the toilets. Surprisingly there were always plenty of hands that went up as some pupils preferred to dig a trench in the school gardens and empty the buckets into it rather than sit through a lesson. One day David recalls a very irate gym mistress who was taking the girls for netball banging on his classroom window protesting that a boy who was emptying the toilets was pushing an overflowing wheelbarrow across her netball court.

Did You Know?

A new 176 place Council School, which opened in 1910, replaced the Wesleyan School of 1854.

School attendance for five to 10-year-olds did not become compulsory until 1870.

The 1870 Education Act involved a parish by parish examination of existing elementary education provision. In Toddington there existed the Toddington National School which could accommodate 153 boys and 151 girls and The Toddington Wesleyan School which could accommodate 198 children

Punishment books were kept as a record of the misdemeanours and punishment dished out to pupils. Girls were generally punished for rudeness, laziness, disobedience or untidiness. Older girls were expected to set a good example to their younger classmates. Punishment used to be by one stroke of the cane on each hand. Boys received harsher punishments than girls. Truancy was a common entry for boys who received six or eight strokes of the cane. All corporal punishments had to be administered by or approved by the headteacher and recorded in the punishment book.

The majority of children, however, wrote on slates, because they were cheap and could be used again and again. At the end of the lesson or when they were full up they would be wiped clean. The pupils would often spit on the slate and wipe it with their sleeve if no sponges were available. The inkwells in the desks would be filled up every morning by the ink monitor. Pens were of poor quality and would regularly leak causing blots on the paper that the pupils would be punished for. Only those in the highest classes were allowed to use pen and paper.

Teachers concentrated on the three R's namely Reading, 'Riting and 'Rithmetic. The teacher would write with chalk onto the blackboard and the pupils would copy or recite the written words. Children were not allowed to speak out of turn and the lessons were very dull. This often resulted in rowdy classes. 'Object' lessons were taught where the pupils would look at an object such as a daisy or a stuffed animal, and discuss and record their observations. However it was easier for teachers to just list information on the object and have the class copy this down. Geography was also taught by chanting or copying down lists of countries or railway stations.

There were frequent complaints about the schoolrooms being too hot, too cold, badly ventilated etc. On winter evenings especially they were too dark.

Reginald Neale, one of the founders of the Toddington Old Boys, was born in Toddington in 1887. He was a pupil-teacher and trained at the pupil-teacher centre in Luton, at the same time being bound apprentice at the Weslyan School, from the age of 14. The Luton centre gave the pupil-teachers instruction and fellowship with one another for, initially, one and a half days a week. At some stage he attended Saltley College, Birmingham, presumably for teacher-training. Only the very best survived the long hours and hard work of a pupil-teachers course. Reginald Neale stated: 'You knew you had to work hard, and in the classroom you had to make it from the start, deciding whether you were to sink or swim. By the time you got to college, you had confidence.

You just knew by then that you could make the grade as a teacher. Nowadays, a man can be trained at college, then find the job is not for him. In my day, that could never have happened.'

Another pupil-teacher was his sister Ella Neale who was trained by Mr Sommerton at the Wesleyan School. She eventually left to give private lessons and later became a teacher at the National School where in 1915 her salary was £50 per annum as an Uncertified Teacher. She continued to teach up to the time of her marriage in 1921.

Mr Sommerton retired in 1932 having being appointed headteacher in 1905 of the Wesleyan School which later became the Council School. On his retirement he commented: 'In the 10 years since the buses came Toddington has been revolutionised. The people instead of being very self-centred have a very much wider outlook. When I first came I used to find that hardly any children had been on a train. But today they are good travellers. They get about east, west, north and south. Toddington is no longer the self centred, isolated place it was.'

Prior to 1944 schools maintained by the Bedfordshire authority were basically two kinds; Elementary, which provided education for children between the ages of 5 and 14 years of age, and Grammar to which entry normally gained at about the age of 11. The 1944 Act required organisation of the statutory system of public education to be in three progressive stages, to be known as primary, secondary and further education.

The General Certificate of Education was introduced in 1951, with its Advanced 'A' level and Ordinary 'O'level. The newspapers at that time complained that the new exams were too hard. In 1959 only 9% of pupils got five O-levels., whereas in 2009, 70% got five A* to C grades at GCSE which was broadly equivalent to O-levels. It wasn't until 1965, when the poorly regarded 'Certificate of Secondary Education' or CSE was introduced, that students at secondary modern schools got any qualifications at all. In reality only 25% of pupils- those at grammar and public schools were offered a proper academic education. In 1986 O-levels were merged with the CSE to make GCSE. All 16-year-olds now took equivalent exams and had the opportunity of obtaining a decent level of education.

In 1967 Beds County Council wanted to pull down the school in Leighton Road. A petition saved the school from demolition and it was used as a home of the village youth club. In 1970 the old school was re-opened and adapted in order to provide two or three extra classrooms. Richard Dillingham said: 'There has not been any overcrowding at the school but the extra classrooms will enable us to reduce the size of classes from about 40 to 25. It will make life very pleasant indeed.' The old school became home to a play school and TADS theatre group before being partly demolished in 1988 to make way for a new village hall.

Above: Senior pupils, 1953-4.
Back row: Jim Wooliscroft, Brian Lawson, David Stamford, Bill Pateman? John Hull.
Front row: Susan Heady, Margaret Jellis , Kathleen Buckingham, Winnie Underwood, Jean Wilson.

Below: Senior pupils, 1955 Back row: Terry Galloway, Michael Ward, Brian Chapman, Tom West or Michael Gale, Harold Giles.
Front row: - , June Harris, Thelma Oakley, Ann Clarke, Daphne Odell.

1957 Netball Team. Back row: Janet Buckingham, Judith Oliver, Linda Lane. Front row: Elizabeth Rogers, Mary Rogers, Rona Kitchiner and Rosemary Bland.

Senior Pupils 1957/8. Back row: -, Mary Rogers, Malcolm Lowe, Rona Kitchiner. Front row: Eric Bowen, Janet Buckingham, Ian Single, -, Dennis Chapman, Yvonne Pasquet .

Football Team, 1958. Back row: Richard Hammond, Philip Emmerton, Donald Nelson, George Chalmers, Peter Fletcher, Jimmy Peck, Tony Jeffreys.
Front row: Derek Lewsey, Ian Russell, Chris Single, Tony Yates, Ian Hanscombe, Martin Edwards.

Senior Pupils, about 1960.

Sports Day, about 1960. Pictured is a wheel-barrow race with Rodney Ilott holding Melvin Shepherd. Below: Shot putter Rodney Ilott in action.

Netball Team 1960.
Back row: Jennifer Fish, - , Marion Peck, Sandra Stringer, Lesley Pasquet.
Front row: Margaret McLellan, Carol Cosgrove, Carol Lane , -

Netball Team 1961.
Back row: Brenda Roberts, Margaret McLellan, Susan Patterson, Carol Lane.
Front row: Susanne Hathaway, Myra Ashby, Linda Heeps.

Football Team, 1961.
Back row: Robinson , Rodney Ilott, Derek Lewsey, - , Bruce Duncan, Brian Northall, Victor Peddar.
Front Row: Keith Smith, - , Melvin Shepherd, Rodney Burman, - , Melvin Edwards, - .

School Choir, about 1961.
Back row: Marian McLellan, Susan Day, Joan Oakley, Susan Mundy, Ann Buckingham, Gwen Cook, Lesley Pasquet, Pam Buckingham and Stella Bainton.
Third row: Diane Hill, Christine Waters, Christine Lane, Margaret McLellan, Shirley Burgoine, Janice Hobbs, Sandra Stringer and Janet Gazeley.
Second row: Rita Kennard, Pat Fairbairn, Jennifer Chandler, Jennie Fish, Lesley Aldred, Margaret Harris, Pauline Justice, Pauline Swain, Kathleen Bainton.
Front row: George Harrison, Alan Turney, Peter Andrews, Stuart Gilbert, Adrian Purser and Robert Burgoine.

Headteacher , John Fewson , on the set of Circus Boy 1961. Pictured behind bars are teachers Mary Malloch, Ena Davies, Sylvia Butler and David Calcott. Mr Fewson was an excellent teacher of Maths and Geography and was happiest when teaching. As the years progressed, excellent results were achieved in external examinations, and as headteacher he made sure personally that each boy or girl was settled into employment when they left school.

Nellie Crump, aged 81 with a glass in her hand, pictured as a guest at the Toddington Old Scholars, March 1980. Nellie used to be the cook at the Council School. Standing: Edna Kent, Priscilla Hart, Beryl Hyde, Margaret Perry, Edna McCarthy.

Headteacher, David Calcott, 2001.

'I started teaching in Toddington at the then Secondary Modern School in September, 1961.At that time it was a comparatively small school and was housed in the building now converted to the Village Hall. A Woodwork room and Art/Music room stood just across from the main building and there was a hall that doubled in the day time as a Science room. There were classrooms also in the Methodist Chapel that stood on the corner of today's Toddington St. George playing field.

In 1961 the school was an 11-15 years school for pupils from Toddington, Harlington and villages in the surrounding area who had not passed the 11-plus examination for a place at one of the local Grammar Schools. There were few academic external examinations in the school at that time and most of the students were prepared for a craft or technical apprenticeship, secretarial work or for some form of manual work. Opportunities to compete with Grammar School students were limited, even for those pupils demonstrating exceptional ability by the time they reached their teens. In spite of these difficulties, however, many of the young people went on to have very successful and rewarding careers.

The headteacher of the school in 1961 was John Fewson. He was a good teacher himself, leading by example, and taught mainly Maths and some Geography. He liked in his words "to run a tight ship" and he had firm ideas as to how pupils and staff had to behave. There were firm but fair rules and a friendly atmosphere pervaded the school.

Some of these rules, however, made staff smile or get very annoyed. All planning books, showing the lesson set out for the whole week, had to be handed to him each Monday and then signed off which seemed to be fair – but when a member of staff wished to have new colouring pencils for the pupils to use these could only be acquired if each box of pencils containing the old stubbs was presented prior to the request.

There was a strict uniform code and pupils and staff were expected to dress "properly"; female pupils and staff were not allowed to wear trousers as an alternative to a dress or skirt and only the PE teacher was allowed the absence of a tie.

In my first term I was amazed when John came into my classroom at break (there was no common room for staff) and confiscated the pipe I was smoking because it was a bad example to the pupils. It was returned on the following Friday. On another occasion he said that if I wore brown shoes instead of black to school again I would "have to go home and change them". A female colleague was indeed sent home for wearing a yellow pair of stockings!

Before the new Secondary School (later to become Middle) was built, possible names were discussed at a staff meeting. Various ideas were suggested but as the school was to be built on fields adjacent to Park Road it seemed more appropriate to recommend the name "Parkfields". This suggestion was accepted and staff and pupils watched the new school being built before it was opened in 1963.

The new school was officially opened by Sir Frederick Mander on the 16 October 1963 and there was much excitement when we moved in and were able to take advantage of the new facilities.

In the 1960s students began to take part in a new examination, the Certificate of Education or CSE. This proved to be a way for many young people to show their academic and practical strengths and to gain basic national qualifications. It showed quickly also that many of the students could pass not only their CSE but also the highly regarded General Certificate of Education or GCE. The school logbooks would show the names of many pupils who passed with very good grades and could compete in terms of qualification with students at grammar and high schools.

During the 1960s and early 1970s, while learning opportunities were increasing, the school was always a happy place where drama, sport, music and other extra-curricular activities could also be enjoyed. There was a flourishing school band and orchestra and twice annually parents could enjoy seeing hundreds of children playing and singing in music concerts. Musicals such as *Calamity Jane*, *South Pacific* and *Oklahoma* were produced; there were performances of Shakespeare's *Macbeth*, *The Merchant of Venice* and *A Midsummer Night's Dream*; the plays, *A Christmas Carol*, *Toad of Toad Hall* and *The Admirable Crichton* played to packed audiences.

There was always a sense of belonging, as much for the young people from Harlington, Eversholt, Chaltton, Tebworth, Milton Bryan, Tingrith and the surrounding villages, as there was for those who lived in Toddington itself.

In 1964 I was awarded a post to write the curriculum timetable; it was a task on which I spent many happy hours over the next 37 years. It seemed that every summer my carpet was littered with small pieces of paper and a large timetable grid.

Like all members of staff in those early years I taught a number of subjects including PE, Maths, History, RE and English. In 1966 I was fortunate enough to be awarded the post of Head of History and the Arts and in 1972 was appointed as Deputy Headteacher. Unfortunately, in the coming months, the headteacher, John Fewson, suffered a heart attack and was often not well enough to come to school; I was given the job of Acting Head in 1973 when sadly, John died. A selfless man, he had worked tirelessly for the school which was his consuming interest.

On 1 April, 1974 I was appointed as headteacher of Parkfields School, a job I would enjoy for the next 27 years. It was a post that was to give me many more successes than disappointments. I never had a real desire to leave at any time and I was happy to work in an environment where there was stability of staffing, both in teaching and in support staff, in an establishment where the great majority of children were eager to learn and which enjoyed the active support of parents.

The 1970s saw the change to comprehensive education and Parkfields became a Middle School for all abilities between the age of nine and thirteen. For the next two decades, free of external examinations, children acquired a whole range of basic skills to equip them for their local Upper School.

The first inspection of Parkfields by the Department for Education and Science, took place in March, 1966. The report concluded as follows; "The school has seized the opportunities offered to it by its excellent new building and is serving the area very well indeed. The Headmaster sets a fine example, which the staff are quick to follow, of treating every pupil as a valuable individual; the pupils in their turn are well-mannered, self-respecting in their bearing, appreciative of their school, and interested in their work. This is a very good school."

There were two further inspections in the 20th century, both conducted by OFSTED. In June, 1994, the main findings of the report concluded: "Parkfields is a good school providing a very sound education for its pupils. Standards are generally high and many pupils are achieving above national norms. Pupils of all abilities are challenged by the work and make good progress. Standards of literacy and numeracy are generally good throughout the school. There is consistency of achievement in both key stages and in all subjects of the curriculum and Parkfields has clearly articulated values which are shared by the school community and supported by the parent body. High standards of behaviour and care for others demonstrate the pupils' development of personal responsibility."

This was followed by a report four years later, in June, 1998, the main findings of which stated: "Pupils at Parkfields School received a very high quality of education. The school has placed a strong emphasis on pupils' personal development, the provision of high-quality care, very high standards of behaviour and breadth of opportunity, particularly for extra-curricular sport and music. Consequently, and justifiably, the school is regarded extremely favourably by parents and the local community. Over the four years they are at the school, pupils make sound progress and maintain good standards, so they are well prepared for the next stage of education."

In 1999, one of the highest awards for school sport, Sportsmark Gold, was presented to the school and was celebrated by the whole school community. I loved to support my school teams when they were competing and the school had many games players, athletes and gymnasts of whom we were proud. Having always played and loved sport myself it was a pleasure to support a variety of sports, even on dark, damp evenings when the boys were playing rugby with such spirit at the Dunstablians Rugby Club.

A number of my parents knew that I enjoyed watching horse racing when I had the time, especially at the big meetings. On many occasions, I was sent a tip for Aintree or Cheltenham or asked for my selection for the Grand National or the Gold Cup. My staff, who of course knew of this interest, presented me on my retirement with tickets for the Cheltenham Festival for the following year, 2002. My wife and I attended the meeting and apart from a thrilling three days, we returned home with a profit!

One of the great satisfactions about being a schoolmaster was the reward that came back many times when former students became successful and one could claim to have had at least a small share in that success. Over three decades, I had the pleasure of welcoming back hundreds of former students, often as parents.

Over the years, Parkfields enjoyed great stability of staffing; the school was fortunate to have had the services of so many talented and conscientious staff, both teaching and non-teaching, and their loyalty was shown in the positive ethos of the school in which they had played such an important part.

It is important to mention the contribution that governors made to Parkfields over many years. Many local people from the school community gave up their time voluntarily to ensure good standards and to create opportunities for local children. Governors not only provided valuable support and advice but, acting with the aims and objectives of the school in mind, were a body of people to whom all who were employed were accountable.

It became a tradition that if you worked at Parkfields, high standards were expected of you and so many children, staff and governors, responded to that challenge.

I retired in 2001 after working in Toddington for forty years, twenty-seven as headteacher of Parkfields School. Teaching for me was a vocation, hard work but always rewarding!'

David Calcott

Pictured at the 50th anniversary are pupils with the former head David Calcott and the present head David Brandon – Bravo.

In May 2013 Parkfields celebrated its 50th anniversary by inviting former pupils and teachers to return to the school to share happy memories and meet old friends. During the day tours of the school were organised. Visitors could look at displays of memorabilia from over the years. Gym, dance and singing performances were given by pupils. In the evening a disco and hog roast took place.

Work commenced on this two-form entry school in September 1961. The school was built at a cost of £136,000 by Messrs J.M. Hill and Sons (Ampthill) Ltd and completed in April, 1963. The County Architect was described as being 'one of the finest architects in the country'.

Built on three levels to follow the natural contours of the site the buildings comprised of eight classrooms, six practical rooms, a combined assembly hall and gymnasium and a library with space for 5,000 to 6,000 volumes. Dominating the view was the village church of St George with 'all the main teaching spaces enjoying a fine vista towards Toddington Parish Church'.

On Wednesday 16 October 1963 Parkfields was officially opened by Sir Frederick Mander. The short service of dedication included passages from the bible read by the head boy and girl. The school choir sang the Twenty-Third Psalm, and everyone joined in the hymn, Now Thank we all our God. *The Rector of Toddington led the prayers and the service ended with the Lord's Prayer and the Grace.*

Before declaring the new school building officially open Sir Frederick spoke about education in general and suggested how important it was that children should get the kind of education for which they are best fitted.

Sir Frederick Mander talked about the 11-plus to the audience. The Luton News *were there to capture his words:*

'I cannot remember any time in my life when such nonsense was talked about the 11-plus. People talk about it, newspapers write about it, as though it is a kind of rat race, a kind of competitive examination, when it is nothing of the kind. It is merely a review of the children in our schools. The object is not to produce passes and failures. I do not think there are many passes and failures in the 11-plus. There should be none. Our sole object is to discover as far as we can what kind of education children are best fitted for, and to see that they get it.

I would like to tell you that in the eyes of Bedfordshire Education Committee all the children in our county are of equal importance. We do not look upon some as better than others. We are not concerned to have the 11-plus to see whether one child is better than another. We try to discover the differences and to cater for those differences to the best of our ability.'

The newspaper stated that as he saw it, the only failure was made by the education authorities by placing a child in a grammar school when he was best fitted for a secondary modern school.

Then prizes for the year were presented by Lady Mander as Speech Day was combined with the opening. The pupils can be seen lining up to receive their prizes.

TO ALL THEIR DUE

GOVERNORS OF THE SCHOOL

1961—1964

CHAIRMAN: Mr. G. D. BABISTER, M.B.E.
VICE-CHAIRMAN: County Councillor D. W. HYDE
County Councillor P. A. Burton
County Councillor L. Rayson
Mr. W. W. Robinson
Mr. F. J. Bonner
Mrs. D. Brinklow
Mr. F. J. Turvey
Mrs. E. M. Lee
Mrs. E. E. Heady
Mrs. D. E. Penrice
Mr. B. J. Hyde

Clerk to the Governors: The Director of Education

MEMBERS OF THE STAFF

Headmaster:
J. W. Fewson

Deputy Head:
Mrs. A. E. Winfield

Assistant Staff:

Mrs. E. Davies, B.A.
Mrs. K. M. Harris
Miss M. K. Malloch
Miss V. A. Perry
Miss P. M. Scott

R. J. Smith (Head of Department)
D. A. E. Calcott
B. Deeley, L.T.C.L.
P. G. Nye
A. E. Sivell, B.Sc.Tech.

Secretary: Mrs. E. Bryant

Cook Supervisor: Mrs. G. N. Kingham

Caretaker: J. Selfe

Groundsman: S. J. Elk

Prize Winners

FORM PRIZES

Form 4	1st	Linda Darton
	2nd	Adrian Purser
	3rd	Alan Turney

Form 3A	1st	Patricia Arnold	*Form 3B*	1st	Carol Morgan
	2nd	Shirley Smith		2nd	Diane Harris
	3rd	Barry Williams		3rd	Lesley Inwards
	Progress	Patricia Pullen		Progress	Barbara Creamer
Form 2A	1st	Philip Stanghon	*Form 2B*	1st	Michael Bird
	2nd	Robert Burden		2nd	Linda Janes
	3rd	Philomena Murphy		3rd	Michael Smith
	Progress	Mary Mountfort		Progress	Robert Edmonds
					Susan Snoxell
Form 1A	1st	Isobel McLellan	*Form 1B*	1st	Michael Niemann
	2nd	Andrew Burnage		2nd	Elaine Harris
	3rd	Christine Anderson		3rd	Sylvia Eves
	Progress	John Williams			

SUBJECT AWARDS

Mathematics	Robert Burden	Brian Day	Patricia Arnold
English	Audrey Roberts		
Woodwork	Alan Turney		
Science	David Chant	Isobel McLellan	
French	Audrey Roberts	Shirley Smith	
Geography	John Wilson		
History	Alex McLellan	Mary Mountfort	
Gardening	Trevor Edwards		
Art	Martin Burnet	Carol Morgan	
Technical Drawing	Philip Parker		

LOYALTY AWARD Pauline Swain

HOUSE POINT WINNERS Mary Mountfort Sylvia Eves Shirley Smith

HOUSE AWARDS

Work	THOMAS	*Rounders*	THOMAS
Football	FOWLER	*Cricket*	FOWLER
Netball	THOMAS		

WILLIAM HYDE AWARDS (*Awarded to the most promising future citizens by the Toddington Old Boys' Association*)

Paul Wilson Ann Neal

Deputy-Head boy, John Wilson, presents a fruit bowl made in the school to Sir Frederick Mander.

Lady Mander presents a prize to Pauline Swain.

The Head Boy, Paul Wilson and Head Girl, Ann Neal pose for the photographer. The school badge reads 'To All Their Due'. Schools in general placed great importance on the wearing of school uniform as it created a sense of pride and belonging.

In September 1963 a Commercial Course was started by nine girls. Twelve months later the following girls had passed the Pitman's typewriting exam: Wendy Bird, Susan Chapman, Susan Cooke, Eveline Michael, Carol Morgan, Marilyn Mort and Susan Underhill.

There were eight Domestic Science units. There was also a small flat where two students would practice at being independent and budgeting for a week. They would wash and clean and cook meals during the week for invited guests. In 2011 a new food technology block was opened.

Ron Smith, Head of Maths taking a Technical Drawing class. The school leaving age was 15 years. For all those that asked for it, there was available an extra year in school. For the academically minded there was the opportunity of sitting for the CSE and other external examinations.

For those in their fourth year the boys could chose between a course with a rural bias and one which concentrated on more technical subjects. For the girls, a two year commercial course was available.

Junior Netball Team, 1964.
Back row: Corrinne Pateman, Helen Michael, Glenda Davis, Pauline Yates, Carol Bandy.
Front Row: Valerie Oakley, Isobel McLellan and Jackie Gordon.

Junior Football Team, 1964.
Back row: Keith Finch, Colin Ballinger, Ian Chalmers, Richard Hobbs and Graham Battams.
Middle row: John Page, Trevor Goble, David Smith, Robert Maycock, Raymond Baker.
Front row: Robin Brewer and Patrick McLaughlin.

School Prefects, 1964. Back row: Marilyn Mort, Susan Chapman, John Wilson, David Chant, Front row: Susan Underhill, Ann Neal, Paul Wilson and Alex McLellan.

Senior Football Team, 1964. Back row: Richard Hobbs, Keith Brinklow, Ian Simmonds, Mervyn Price, Aubrey Russell, Alex McLellan, Stan Coles.
Front row: Kevin Upton, Paul Wilson, John Wilson, Barry Rowles, Brian Horne?

School Clubs

These met during the dinner break, after school or in the evenings.

The Angling Club was run by Mr Calcott and they met every week on Wednesdays. After school fishing took place at the canal at Slapton or Leighton Buzzard. In the holidays a mini-bus was hired to go further afield.

The Dancing Club met every Thursday evening where pupils learnt the Waltz, Quickstep, Cha Cha , The Gay Gordons and the Dashing White Sergeant. Over 120 pupils attended the Valentine Dance in 1964. In the same year a competion was held for which silver cups were awarded to Robert Burden partnered by Linda Izinger, and to Dennis Fuller with Pauline Swain as his partner.

The Gym Club was run by Mr Nye and later by Mr Hinchcliffe. 'The point of the club was to help those boys who found Physical Training difficult and for the boys to enjoy it.'

For the girls there was the **Flower Arranging Club** run by Mrs Harris . This also attracted a few boys for in the Autumn Competion 'a few boys entered and did quite well'. However the girls shone and Julie Powis was first, and Patricia Crowe second.

There was also a **Cine Club** and **Badminton Club** not to mention the **School Band**. The first band practice with Mr Hyde was held on the 17 January 1964. The first tunes played were the *National Anthem*, *Now the Day is Over* and *Au Clair de la Lune*. On cornets were Penelope Bartalis, Tina Stapleton, Malcolm Quick, Patrick McLaughlin, Kenneth Pirrie and Michael Clark. On horns were Michael Aldred, Peter Jeffries and Philip Stanghon. Desmond Hopwood and Robert Swain were on trombones whilst Ronald McDaid was on bass.

Saving up for big items like bicycles was actively encouraged at home. When Mary Mountfort, aged 14, wanted a pony her parents actively encouraged her to save the money. They agreed to contribute one-third of the cost provided Mary found the other two-thirds. The pony would cost between £50 and £100 and Mary had a Dimple Haig Whisky bottle full of sixpences, which when full, held about £35. Her story appeared in the school magazine in 1964:

'To help me raise money for my pony I have some battery hens. With the profit from the hens I have bought two calves which I am weaning, and fattening on barley, to produce the popular barley beef. If any money is gained from my calves it will go towards my savings. I have also given up my comics for "Flicka" my pony to be. As well as saving money I am collecting useful items for grooming a pony. When showing cows at Shows I have collected various oddments needed, for example, a dandy brush, hoof pick, and a water brush. It will cost me about ten shillings a week to keep Flicka in the summer and fifteen to twenty shillings in the winter. This money I plan to pay by having a paper round, and from my pocket money.'

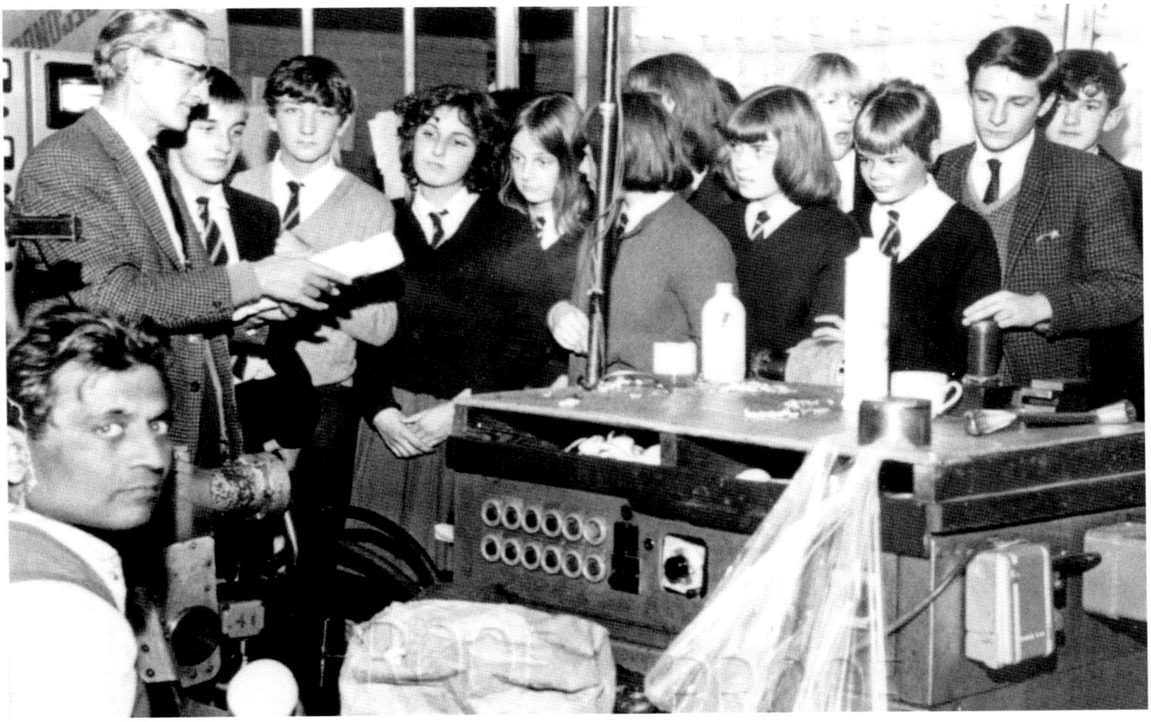

From time to time visits were made to local industry to give pupils an idea of what jobs were available when they left school.

Brass instruments being played by pupils.

Football Team, 1967-8. Back row: Malcolm Soper, Ian Knowles, Raymond Baker, Steve Buckingham, Charlie Rogers, - , Peter Jefferies.
Front row: Ian Stewart , Graham Burman, Richard Hobbs, - , Roger Dryden.

One of the eight Domestic Science units, 1960s.

School production of Toad of Toad Hall, *January 1968.*

School production of Calamity Jane, *December 1968.*

285 Production of South Pacific, *Xmas 1969.*

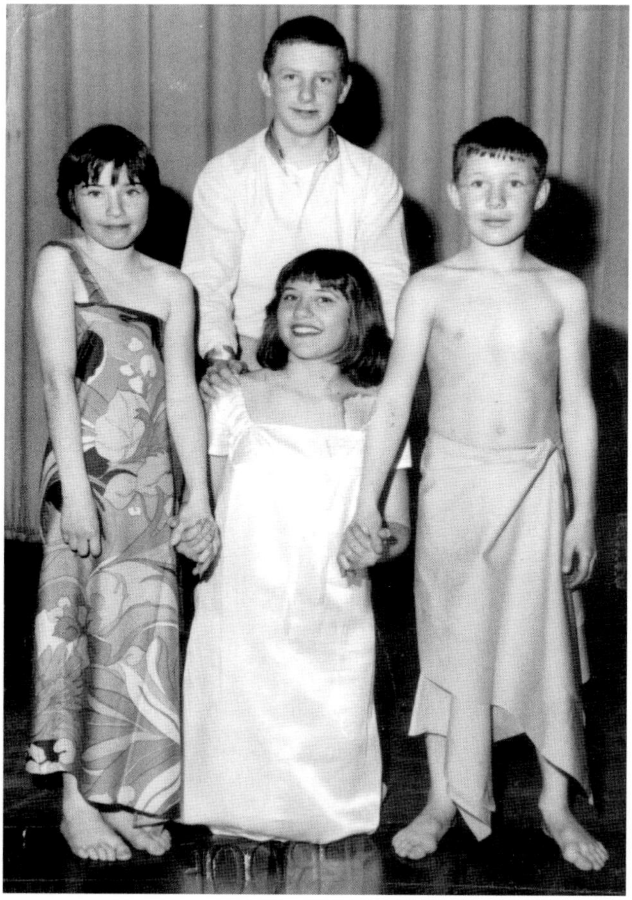

Back row: Ian Kennard
Front row: Janet Audley, -, Keith Clark.

Prefects 1966-67 pictured outside the classrooms on the school playing field.
Back row: Ian Knowles, David Cook, Richard Hobbs, Raymond Baker, Teresa Toone, Janice Brown, Janet Green, Lynda Austin.
Middle row: Sharp , Andrew Burnage , Isobel McLellan, (Head Girl); Robert Maycock, (Head Boy); Elaine Harris, Tina Anderson.
Front row: Roger Dryden, Charles Rogers, Christine Smith, Valerie Coles.

There were four houses namely Fowler (red), Thomas (green), Cleaver (blue) and Hyde (yellow). The houses might have been named after the first three chairmen and the founder of the Toddington Old Boys Association. There were also football and netball house matches where each house team played one another. Sports Day bought more competition between the houses with each competitor competing for their particular house. Today the houses have been renamed: Pankhurst (red), Austen (green), Churchill (yellow) and Scott (blue). In this sack race Carol Bandy is out in front.

Teacher, David Calcott smoking his pipe, with a class of fifth year pupils, 1960s. Occasionally he would set his class a historical quiz based on the Hughie Green television show Double Your Money. Instead of money pupils played for house points. Called "Double Your House Points" every time a pupil answered a question correctly their house points doubled. The questions got harder as points accumulated. Get a question wrong and they lost everything. No one ever won!

Sonnie Wing recalls the day David Calcott joined:

'I remember being a prefect on hall duty on the day that David Calcott arrived. David came into the hall at the Secondary Modern School and I sort of studiously walked up to him and said "Can I help you?" He said "Yes, I'm the new teacher." So I said "Oh really, I suppose I'd better show you to the Headmaster's study then." So I duly did so and then about five minutes later John Fewson arrived. We were all a little frightened of Mr Fewson so I squared up to him in an official sort of way and said "Mr Fewson the new teacher has arrived". "Oh he told you he was the new teacher did he!" I thought "Oh my God I have said something a little bit wrong there".'

Sports Day, 1970s.

A school class poses for the photographer, about 1976. Donna Constable is seated front centre.

The last Fifth Form at Parkfields Secondary School, 1976. Pictured back row: David Warner, Brown, Ian Smith, Paul Harris (deputy head) , David Calcott (head), Phil Bennett and Graham McDonald.

A cross-country run for the boys and girls across Conger field, about 1978. Starting from Parkfields the runners ran down past Conger Hill, then returned up the muddy path at the bottom of Conger Lane and finished on the Green. Debbie Welland can be seen centre front below.

Historian and former builder Victor Seymour explains to pupils the history of Toddington with the aid of a model of the village.

Its head down and no talking in this classroom. School leaves a lasting impression. We never forget the friends we made, the teachers who taught us and the rules we broke.

Music lesson with percussion instruments. Tambourines, xylophones, drums and maracas can be seen.

A qualified teacher of the deaf with children who have a range of hearing losses ranging from moderate, severe to profound. They are in a small classroom fitted with teaching aids. The room is suited for small classes of up to six learners. This special Learning Support Unit was set up in the 1974 to take in pupils with learning difficulties from miles around.

Teachers and pupils present a leaving present to Mary Malloch, who taught typing, shorthand and maths at the school. She retired in 1988 after 25 years service. She was acting deputy head for the last 18 months of her career. Mary joined the staff in September 1961. She told a Luton News *reporter: 'I was at the old Leighton Road building then. The children used to have to get coal in to heat the place up, and we used to take our dinners into the classroom to eat. When I first joined it was a secondary modern school, now it's for nine to 13s. There was a tremendous lot of children at the school at one time-it actually went up to 600 at one stage. Now there's about 350 but once there was just 200 and you knew everyone.'*

Former pupil Helen Twelvetrees (1975-1979) recalls how Mrs Malloch used to stand at the back of the assembly hall as the students filed in: 'She could always identify you from the back of your head if you messed about and the whole school would know about it.'

Parkfields Middle School Staff 1993/4.
Back row: Susie Bay (clerical asst), Sue Elwes (admin.asst), Pat Offer (P/E), David Holmes (R/E) , Neil Janes, (site agent), Ken Hester (head of year 7/Maths), Andy Fisher (P/E).
Third row: Dee Curtis (p/t RE), Claire Meigh (librarian), Yvonne Burrows (medical), Lindy Morrison (year 5 teacher), Ivan Holgate (CD/IT), Louise Monk (lab asst), Dave Fisher (Science).
Second row: Nick Sharpe (head of year 6 Hist/Geog), Sheila Fern (Art), Cath Tomlinson (Hist/Geog), Jenny Hudson (French), Brenda Keen (Maths), Jane Pitts (English), Andra Bishop,(p/t misc), Angela French (CD).
Front row: Iris Taylor (school secr), Jan Webb (French/Learning Support), Dave Harper (Deputy Head), David Calcott (Headteacher), Rick Fern (head of year 5), Carolyn O'Donnell (head of year 8 /English), Judith Cunningham (Science).

Former Manchester United and England footballer Bobby Charlton pictured with Parkfield Middle School pupils, Natalie Rose, Debbie Graham, Paul Mayhew and Chris Brook at Luton Regional Sports Centre, 1991.

February 2001, skiing trip to Austria.

French exchange to Oise, near Paris, Easter 2001.

Sports day , 2001. Charlotte Gurr and Peter Young are pictured centre.

Steph Hill, Jade Christie, Emily Randall and Jenna show their cheeky side to the photographer.

Staff pictured July 2001.
Back row: Cath Tomlinson, Ruth Murphy, Sue Teague , Jane Pitts, Jan Webb.
Middle row: Jan Sylvester , Claire MacGregor, Angela French, Ivan Holgate, Debbie Nicholls, Lindy Morrison, Rachael Bendefy .
Front row: Lorna Vivian, Kate Masssink, Andra Bishop, Pat Offer, David Calcott, Rick Fern, Andrew Fisher, David Holmes, Annie Botfield.

Parkfields Middle School, May 2005. Pictured back row are Hannah Bodsworth, headteacher David Brandon-Bravo, deputy head Nick Sharpe, Chris Horncastle. Front row: Emily Chennell-Clarke, Martin Stanford, David Dove, Tegan Metters, Nicola Fowler, Adam Sells.

In the 2004 Ofsted report it was stated: 'This is a very good school whose headteacher, senior managers, governors and staff have created an effective and warm learning environment.' The report went on to say that the quality of teaching was very good with one in five lessons being outstanding. The headteacher, Mr Brandon-Bravo was singled out for praise. The report stated that the quality of his leadership was 'very good with many outstanding features'. The governing body was described as being 'very good' and with their help the headmaster had created a 'warm and happy learning environment'.

Headteacher David Brandon-Bravo contributed this article in April 2006 to the *Toddington and District Newsletter*:

'Once children finish their schooling at St Georges they usually move into Parkfields Middle School. Parkfields is located at the back of St Georges in Park Road. Parkfields also has a Hearing Impaired Unit allowing children to progress smoothly from one school to another. Children will continue their education here at Parkfields until the age of 13 when they will be in Year 8.

The school has standards above both the county averages and well above the national averages in Maths, English and Science. Children have the opportunity to lead a very full and varied life at the school both during and out of school hours. The school employs (through the County) a number of peripatetic music teachers allowing children to continue learning (if they were playing at their lower school) or to begin learning a selection of musical instruments. These include the guitar, woodwind, brass, drums, and strings. The school has its own band which meets once a week after school, and is involved along with the children who have music lessons in the school, in performing to parents.

Children at school enjoy a wide variety of sporting activities, which change each term. Rugby, cross country, football, netball and hockey tend to be taught during the autumn and spring terms along with dance, basketball and gym. In the summer the children learn to play tennis and take part in various athletics activities. The school takes part in many interschool competitions, has a reputation for performing well and has many trophies to be proud of.

There are many lunchtime clubs that the children can choose to join. These include sign language, chess, various sports, ICT, singing, English, sewing, Christian Youth club and the Green Team (environmental). The curriculum is enhanced through links with external visitors coming into school including various theatre companies, sports clubs, science workshops, representatives from the fire and police force and various speakers who visit individual classes or whole school assemblies.

External visits add significant weight to the areas covered in school. Trips are organised in line with the subjects being covered in the curriculum and are extremely varied. Visits have included Woburn Abbey (science related), a Hindu mosque, a Sikh temple, local churches, Hazard Alley (a safety centre), the Science Museum, Natural History Museum and theatres to see musicals, plays and pantomimes. At the end of the summer term the children have the chance to enjoy a fun trip to end the year – this could include Legoland, Drayton Manor, Knebworth House or Warwick Castle.

When the children start their second year (Year 6) at Parkfields they can enjoy a weekend away at an activity centre which builds on social skills and the ability to work together through a selection of activities both indoors and outdoors. In Year 7 children have the opportunity to attend a longer course which tends to be more of a geographical field trip with some additional (fun) activities at the end of the day.

All children have the opportunity to join a skiing trip which takes place over the February half term. Parents also have the chance to join the children. The children like to be involved with the local community and enjoy singing carols on the green at Christmas, hold a Christmas party for senior citizens and collect harvest gifts for members of the community. The school has strong links with local services including the police, health service and local sports clubs.

Each year group elects representatives to join the school council which plays an active role in bringing ideas and improvements to fruition. If you would like to visit the school to get more of a flavour for the learning environment we offer, or if you are interested in becoming involved as a governor or helper please get in touch.'

In 2013 the school had on average 480 pupils aged between nine and thirteen. There are four main feeder lower schools, but in the 2012 intake the school took pupils from no fewer than 18 lower schools. The school motto is 'to flourish, learn and grow' and together with their Trust Partners they have taken over the county provision for deaf children. In the 2012 Inspection Report it was stated that among its awards the school had Sportsmark Gold, the International School Award and National Healthy School Status.

Staff in April 2013:

Mrs L. Anchor
Mrs J. Bailey
Mrs L. Bodsworth
Mrs S. Bollins
Mrs A. Botfield
Mr A. Boyle
Mrs S. Bracey
Mr D. Brandon-Bravo
Mrs S. Brandon-Bravo
Dr J. Breed
Mrs J. Britton
Mrs P. Broderick
Miss A. Burrows
Mrs Y. Burrows
Mr J. Burt
Mrs M. Cao
Mrs K. Carter
Mrs E.Cavalier
Mrs J. Challis
Mrs K. Chesterton
Mrs P. Collins
Mrs S.Conder
Mrs S.Cooper
Mrs J. Day
Mrs C. Doerr
Mrs T. Doyle
Mrs D. Farley
Mrs J. Fishenden
Mr A. Fisher
Mrs L. Gough
Mr R. Green
Mrs R. Groves
Mrs J. Harper
Mrs J. Hopcroft
Mrs L. Horn
Mrs P. Howe
Mrs C. Ireson
Mrs B. Jackson
Mr N. Janes
Mrs E. Johnstone
Mrs H. Kay
Mrs V. Kearns
Mrs F. Killinger
Mrs D. King
Mrs V. Lake
Mrs C. MacGregor
Mrs J. Major
Mrs J. Manners
Mrs S. McLaughlin
Mrs C. McNeil
Mrs L. Minshull
Mrs L. Monk
Mrs L. Moore
Mrs J. Morley
Miss L. Murton
Mrs D. Nicholls
Mrs S. Nicols
Mrs R. O'Dell
Miss J. Parrish
Mrs C. Phillips
Mrs R. Porzio
Mrs A. Pullan
Mr A. Purdom
Mr S. Purdom
Mrs T. Reidy
Mrs F. Reynolds
Mrs D. Ring
Mrs G. Roberts
Mr G. Roberts
Mrs C. Robinson
Mrs D. Scott
Mrs K. Sear
Mrs J. Sewell
Mrs J. Smith
Mr D. Soper
Mrs T. Stanford
Mrs M. Steadman
Miss G. Tough
Mr I. Tyrie
Mrs T. Williamson
Mrs P. Wren
Mrs H. Wright